ALWAYS SOMETHI

ALWAYS SOMETHING DOING

A History of Boston's Infamous SCOLLAY SQUARE

David Kruh

1990

Faber and Faber

Boston and London

Cover Photo: Scollay Square in 1947 (Courtesy of Robert Stanley).

Copyright © 1989 by David S. Kruh

Library of Congress Cataloging-in-Publication Data
Kruh, David S.
    Always something doing : a history of Boston's infamous Scollay
Square / by David S. Kruh.
        p.   CM.
    ISBN 0-571-12911-0 : $14.95
    1. Scollay Square (Boston, Mass.) — History. 2. Scollay Square
(Boston, Mass.) — Pictorial works. 3. Boston (Mass.) — History — 1865-
4. Boston (Mass.) — Description — Views. 5. Urban renewal-
-Massachusetts — Boston — History — 20th century. I. Title.
F73.65.K78   1990   89-48497
974.4'61 — dc20   CIP

Design by Nancy Dutting
Printed in the United States of America

CONTENTS

7

Let's go and have one "all around" as we visit the most
popular eatery in the Square.

8

An attempt to complete the scrapbook.

9

The hows, the whys, and the results of urban renewal.

10

From musicals to comic books, some people refuse to let
the Square die.

This book is dedicated to
the three most important people in my life:
my mother, Gladys, who always believed
I would succeed, no matter what;
my father, Louis, who always told me I could
achieve anything I wanted as long as I
approached it with tenacity and hard work;
my wife, Mauzy, for giving me the support
I needed to prove that they were both right.

ACKNOWLEDGMENTS

My deepest thanks to the following people for helping to make this book possible. The quality I hope is in it could not have been achieved without their help and support:

The Boston Public Library Microfilm Department, Leo Ajemian, Leo Ajemian, Jr., Phil Bergan and the staff of the Bostonian Society, Red Buttons, Eddie Calmus, John Collins, Ann Corio, Joan Dalton, Joe Flashman, Mayor Ray Flynn, Paula Fontaine and the Spotlighters Club, Mrs. George Gloss, Ken Gloss, Ed Insogna and the whole Joe & Nemo's family, Dr. Henry Kaplan, Louis Kruh, Fred Langone, Ed Logue, Dan McCole of the *Boston Herald*, Ettie McKay, Fred McLellan, Dick Mulligan of the B.R.A., "Dapper" O'Neil, Paula Posnick and the staff of the West End Boston Public Library, Frank and Dorothea Reed, George Sanborn of the M.B.T.A. Library, Ralph Saya, Dick Sinnot, Charlie Speliotis, Robert Stanley, Larry Storch, Jack Thomas of the *Boston Globe*, Alan Tolz, Mike Tredeau, Daniel Van Buskirk, and Jerry Williams of WRKO radio.

My thanks, too, to everyone not mentioned by name who took the time to talk about Scollay Square and who helped me feel as if I, too, was there. After talking with all of you, I wish that I could have been,

I want to take this opportunity to thank Faber and Faber for taking a chance on *Always Something Doing*. They believed, as I had for the past six years, that the story of Scollay Square deserved to be told. The staff, through its professionalism and support, has made this, my first foray into publishing, an enjoyable learning experience. My gratitude to Betsy Uhrig for a great job of editing.

Finally, to Dr. Ellis Johnson of the State University College at Cortland for getting me started; thanks, Doc.

INTRODUCTION

A heavy lead ball dangled menacingly at the end of a crane sitting on Howard Street. A large crowd of people had gathered in the heart of Scollay Square, the city's infamous entertainment district, on this June day in 1961 to watch the end of an era in Boston. Just an hour or two ago they had seen a three-alarm fire destroy the interior of the 116-year-old Howard theater. Now they would watch the city tear the rest of it down.

Slowly, the crane operator began to move the cab back and forth, causing the ball at the end of the cable to swing. It soon etched out a giant arc across the street, grazing the walls of the still smoldering building. With one last swivel, the ball took a final warm-up swing. Its arc was interrupted by the first impact with the granite front of the renowned burlesque theater. Large chunks of masonry fell to the ground. In the street below, some people winced as the crane reared back for another strike.

As the crane continued its work the crowd was silent. What could anyone say? "Progress" had won again, and with its victory another piece of the city's past would come down. But wait . . . something was happening. Actually, something was *not* happening. The crane had been knocking away at the same section of the theater's wall three or four times, yet the wall still stood! It seemed that the Old Howard wasn't going to give up without a fight.

The crane operator tried attacking the wall several more times, but the wrecker was unable to finish the deed, and the crane trundled away. The Old Howard had won a stay of execution, if only a short one. It would take sticks of dynamite to dislodge the huge granite supports from their century-old resting place. Eventually the theater, along with the rest of Scollay Square, succumbed to urban renewal and was bulldozed away.

Where Is Scollay Square?

Today, there is little to mark the site of old Scollay Square, home of burlesque shows and bars, tattoo parlors and hot dog stands, other than a few streets signs and a subway stop. These are located in Boston at Government Center, a collection of city, state, federal, and privately owned buildings constructed under the umbrella of urban renewal during the 1960s. This area is the very heart of the city, close to the State House, Court House, and retail shopping districts, including the refurbished Quincy Market.

When the Government Center project razed Scollay Square it also demolished, altered, or moved several smaller, less notorious squares. Because of its notoriety, Scollay Square has been the focus of everyone's attention during and since demolition; the name had long been used to describe not just the original intersection of Court and Tremont streets, but all of the streets, squares, and alleyways between Beacon Hill and Faneuil Hall. The rest of the area was left to change or disappear without any fanfare. The irony here is that all but one of these squares — Pemberton — existed for almost two hundred years before Scollay Square came into being.

It was said of Scollay Square, because it was so congested with these smaller squares and alleyways, that tourists attempting to traverse it often ended up where they started. To prevent your own confusion, here is a quick survey of the area.

Dock, Adams, and Haymarket squares, located near Faneuil Hall and Quincy Market, were to the north and east of Government Center. At one time they flourished with hundreds of stores, shops, and open-air markets which fed off the enormous activity generated by a healthy Boston Harbor. Dock Square is now a simple intersection near Faneuil Hall, and Adams Square is buried beneath the new City Hall. Haymarket Square is a transit stop for buses and subways.

Brattle Square, a collection of small businesses in the center of the project area, was replaced by the sea of red brick in front of City Hall, known as City Hall Plaza. Pemberton Square, to the west and just above Scollay Square on Beacon Hill, still exists today, but without the cluster of buildings that used to surround the old courthouse it is barely recognizable to anyone who hasn't been around Boston in thirty years. Finally, Bowdoin Square, which contained mostly small businesses and theaters, was, except for the New England Telephone building, completely demolished in the late fifties and early sixties and replaced by private and government office buildings.

Bowdoin Square marks the northwestern edge of Government Center and also represents the beginning of another part of Boston changed by urban development — the West End, a mostly residential neighborhood between Scollay Square, Beacon Hill, North Station, and the Charles River. It was home to thousands of people who were evicted in 1958, when their homes were replaced by costly high-rise apartments.

The West End

The West End deserves special discussion before we begin our look at Scollay Square because, unlike the North End and Beacon Hill (which also bordered the Square), its residents considered Scollay Square a part of their neighborhood. When the city held a public ceremony in 1987 to restore the name Scollay Square to what, twenty-five years earlier, had been christened Government Center, hundreds of West Enders showed up, making the event something of a reunion.

Why do the West Enders feel such a bond with Scollay Square? One reason might be the almost simultaneous destruction of both, cementing together these two parts of Boston in their minds. Another reason has to do with the location of the West End and Scollay Square with respect to the rest of the city. There's an old joke whose punchline comes from a New England native telling a tourist, "You can't get there from here." Because the West End was separated from the center of Boston by Scollay Square, for West Enders that punchline might have been re-worded, "You can't get there from here—without going through Scollay Square." Because of this geography, Scollay Square's streets would have been as familiar to West End residents as their own block.

But this familiarity did not breed contempt. Rather, you will find in this book a remarkable consistency in the West Enders' recollections of Scollay Square. While they all agreed that the Square in its heyday was bawdy, filled with huck-sters, bookies, sailors, and drunks, they were unanimous in their assessment that this place was safe to walk through at any time of the day or night, for men, women, even children. It is hard, I suppose, for those of us who live in or near a major city like Boston to understand this apparent contradiction, but then it is also difficult for us to fathom an inner-city neighborhood where people scrubbed the sidewalks in front of their apartments.

Always Something Doing is not a personal memory of Scollay Square, as I am too young to know it as anything but Government Center. A large portion of the book, therefore, rests upon the memories of older Bostonians who remember the Square from their youth. And many of the people quoted here came from the West End.

It is difficult enough, when researching a topic that relies so much on personal memory, to separate history from nostalgia. The plight of the West Enders made this task even more difficult, since their memories of Scollay Square are often such bittersweet blends of the playground that the rest of Boston knew and the home that was taken away from them. Perhaps then, it is understandable that they some-times seem to glorify what to the rest of us may have seemed rundown or mun-dane. To them, Scollay Square was home.

By examining the Square from this perspective we can see why many older resi-dents of Boston (not just the West Enders but those from the North End, Dor-chester, and other Boston neighborhoods) are quick to tell anyone who will listen that there was something special about Scollay Square beyond the hot dogs, the bars, and the burlesque shows. It is a feeling that runs deep as they watch their city's agonizing battle with drugs, poverty, and indifference: that the passing of Scollay Square also represented the passing of an era when, perhaps, life in America really was kinder and gentler.

Why Scollay Square

So why *was* this collection of bars and theaters so special? That's the first thing I asked my fellow Bostonians after moving here from New York in 1981. A conversation with an uncle who had served aboard a destroyer during the Second World War had piqued my curiosity, and I came to Boston wanting to know more. I found out quickly that if you ask a Boston-area resident over a certain age about this place, you are bound to get a smile. Faking a stomach virus and leaving high school for a day in the Square was so common that it's surprising the activity didn't end up as part of the basic curriculum.

This streak of insubordination seems to have run throughout the population, whether someone grew up on Beacon Hill and enrolled in prep school, or lived elsewhere and attended public school, from the late 1800s right up until the closing of the Old Howard in 1953. Yet despite their brazen acts of truancy, many of these scofflaws eventually became successful lawyers, doctors, accountants, policemen, city councillors, mayor, governor, and even President.

What these young men and women were skipping school to visit was a place completely unique in America. Located within its borders were tattoo parlors, burlesque houses, hot dog stands, photography studios, nightclubs, restaurants, and one of the most famous theaters in the country, the Howard Athenaeum, where just about everyone who ever made it big in vaudeville, burlesque, or radio performed at one time or another.

Until now, the story of Scollay Square has never been fully told: for while it starts off in very traditional Boston style with Puritans in drab frocks, it ends with strippers in front of footlights wearing nothing but tassels and G-strings. Is it any wonder that the city that prides itself as the home of the American Revolution relegates this part of its past to a footnote? Unfortunately, lost among the tassels in Scollay Square are acts of Revolutionary War bravery, entrepreneurial skill and cunning, medical and scientific advances, and the courage of Americans who fought on the side of equality and justice for people of all colors. This book presents two sides of Scollay Square's past: a combination of personal anecdotes and documented "George Washington slept here" historical facts. It is appropriate that a city so rich in history can lay claim to both types existing in the same place.

1

Scollay Square and Its Place in History

We start off with something of a prehistory of Scollay Square, as this name was not officially given to this section of Boston until more than two hundred years after the first settlers made their homes here. It was during the first two centuries of Boston's existence that a wonderful collection of medical pioneers, real estate entrepreneurs, patriots, loyalists, preachers, and strange public servants started building the legend that would become Scollay Square.

Puritan Boston

When a group of English settlers led by John Winthrop came to Boston in 1630, they found an isthmus precariously connected to the rest of Massachusetts. Located on this tadpole-shaped piece of land (which the Indians had named Shawmut) were three mountains, which the settlers dubbed the Tri-mountains.

Three years later the Reverand John Cotton arrived from England, where he had fled arrest by religious authorities for nonconformity. Arriving in Boston in September 1633, he obtained an acre and a half at the base of the tallest of the Tri-mountains. The Cotton estate was located just south of where Pemberton Square would someday lie, on the site of the Suffolk County Savings Bank in Scollay Square. (Today it would be located under Three Center Plaza, a private office building.) Cotton became minister of the first church in Boston and the city's spiritual leader. The hill on which he settled was soon named in his honor.

Cotton Hill

Cotton's property served several prominent citizens over the years, among them Henry Vane. A governor of Massachusetts and a member of the Town Court, Vane lived with John Cotton from 1635 to 1637 before returning to England. There, in 1662, Vane became Scollay Square's only resident on record to be imprisoned in the Tower of London. Following the restoration of Charles II to the throne, he was executed for failing to take the oath of loyalty to the crown.

Later, in 1689, Cotton's property passed to Judge Samuel Sewall, who served on the bench during the witchcraft trials of 1692. Sewall's notoriety comes from his actions following the trials when, much to the consternation of a few citizens, he granted reprieves to some of the victims of that hysteria.

South (and just below) the Cotton estate was the home of Richard Bellingham. He was both deputy governor and governor of the Massachusetts Bay Colony four times from 1641 to 1665, but is probably best remembered for his rather interesting behavior. In fact, considering what has transpired in Scollay Square since his time, Governor Bellingham is a fitting beginning.

At the age of fifty Bellingham became a widower. One day a boarder in Bellingham's home came to the governor to ask him to perform a marriage ceremony. The young man's fiancée was a beautiful woman named Penelope Pelham. Smitten by her looks, Bellingham somehow managed to convince her to marry him instead! He performed the ceremony himself. As was the law at the time, a couple had to publish banns, or public declarations of marriage proposals. Bellingham, in his haste to marry the young Penelope, had not taken the time to do this and was immediately charged with failing to publish his banns. He quickly pointed out that as governor he would sit as judge and jury on any trial held on his case, assuring one and all that his wedding to Miss Pelham would stand. The matter was dropped.

Some time later the governor had a woman put to death as a witch, although there was very little evidence to convict her of the crime. (The poor woman *was* guilty of being Bellingham's sister-in-law and a vocal critic of his administration.)

Next to Bellingham's estate was the home of the schoolmaster Daniel Maud. America's first public school, the Boston Latin Academy, held classes in Maud's home on Tremont street from 1636 until 1642. (Now located in another part of the city, Boston Latin is one of the most prestigious high schools in the country.)

Other denizens of Cotton Hill included John Endecott, who also served as governor of the colony four times during the 1600s. The Reverend John Davenport lived on the hill in 1637 before setting off, along with others, to found the city of New Haven, Connecticut. South of Bellingham's property lived the first shopkeeper in Boston, John Coggan. (Several generations later Coggan's half-acre estate came into the hands of Dr. John Jeffries, a Harvard-educated doctor and loy-

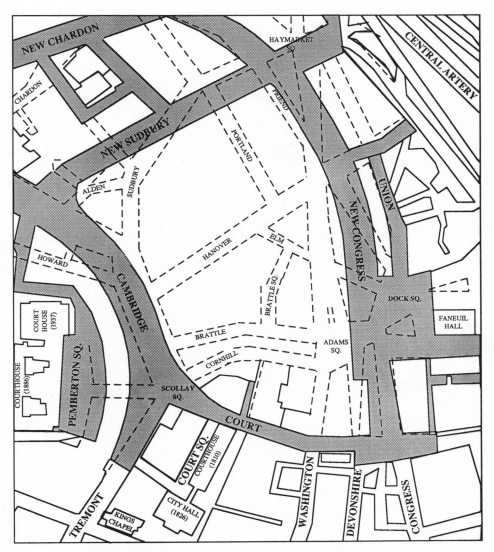

Adapted from a B.R.A. map of the Government Center project area, this map shows what happened to the twenty-two streets that once made up Scollay Square. The large open space in the middle of the map now contains Boston's City Hall and the John F. Kennedy federal building (Daniel VanBuskirk).

alist, who fled Boston in 1776. His unique accomplishment was that he twice flew over the English Channel in a balloon, a remarkable feat for the day.)

Elihu Yale lived on Cotton Hill until the age of four, when his family moved to England. He made his fortune trading with the Far East, but established his place in American history by bestowing large gifts of money to a new college getting started in New Haven. The college, in turn, took his name for its own. (Today, if you visit the site of Cotton Hill you will find yourself in the walled-in, concrete canyon called Pemberton Square. There you can see two weathered plaques placed there in 1930 during the city's tricentennial celebration. One indicates the place where John Cotton's home stood. The other plaque marks the spot where Governor Endecott lived and where Yale was born.)

On the southern part of what used to be Governor Bellingham's property, trader and merchant Andrew Faneuil built a home in 1710. The three-story mansion was elegantly appointed on the inside, while outside there were stables, landscaped terraced gardens, the city's first hothouse, and a gazebo. The property was inherited by Andrew's son Peter in 1738. Peter Faneuil was another successful merchant, who believed in expressing his gratitude to the city that had made him so prosperous. In 1742, he bestowed on the city a two-story building near the water's edge at Dock Square for use as a town hall and marketplace.

The very next year Peter Faneuil died of dropsy at age forty-three. Tragically, the first meeting that took place in the new town hall was Faneuil's funeral. A short time later the city named the structure after him and today Faneuil Hall (part of the renovated Quincy Market project) still serves the public in much the same way it did over two hundred years ago, as a marketplace and meeting hall.

Boston Looks for a Good Time

Along with the prosperity that prompted Faneuil, Yale, and others to public acts of generosity came the other side of success. As wealth spread through the population, so did the need for amusement. It was only natural that the dockhands, laborers, clerks, craftsmen, and other workers would seek ways to enjoy their leisure time and spend their hard-earned money in pursuit of pleasurable activities. They couldn't spend their money at the theater, because plays, concerts, and dance recitals were banned in the city. The rich chose to emulate English society by holding teas and dinner parties, but the dockhands were looking for more than tea and crumpets after unloading a frigate.

A look at the transcript of the General Court of Massachusetts from 1650 reveals one popular leisure activity. Court officers were very disturbed, according to the document, by the "lewd and drunken behavior of sailors on leave." Imagine that! The city was only twenty years old and sailors were already creating a stir trying to have a good time.

With that in mind, it should come as no surprise to learn of another flourishing part of Boston's economy. Walter Muir Whitehill relates this line about the city from an English army officer's 1775 journal: "No such thing as a play house, they were too puritanical a set to admit of such lewd Diversions, tho' ther's perhaps no town of its size cou'd turn out more whores than this could" (*Boston: A Topographical History*, 1968). The size of this population is perhaps best demonstrated by the fact that by the mid-1700s the western slope of Mount Vernon (the western side of Beacon Hill and the third of three mountains on the original isthmus), was designated on several maps as Mount Whoredom.

So the elements that eventually came together to make Scollay Square the bawdy place that Boston loved were present almost from the beginning of the city's history. This despite the ever-present and vigilant watch of its Puritan fathers. Further complicating the Puritans' task in the late seventeenth century was a loosening of the theological monopoly they had held over Boston since its founding. In what is recognized as a major break with conservative Puritanism, a new church was formed in 1699 in what would soon be part of Scollay Square — Brattle Square.

Brattle Square

Brattle Square was originally a passageway from Court Street, which ran along the base of Beacon Hill, to the garden of citizen Joseph Belknap. Today this path would cut across City Hall Plaza from Two Center Plaza to the base of City Hall. It became an official street (called Hillier's Lane) in the late 1600s. Through a series of sales and inheritances, Thomas Brattle, who was treasurer of Harvard University, got title to the property, which he named Brattle Street.

In 1697 a group of Bostonians, many of them well-to-do merchants and tradesmen who were tired of the confining nature of the Puritan service, met to discuss plans for a new church. In January of 1698, Thomas Brattle deeded to them a piece of land called Brattle Close, which was located in the center of his property. The next year they built a wooden meeting house on the site, selected a preacher, and published a declaration of principles which they titled "A Manifesto or Declaration, set forth by the undertakers of the new church, Now Erected in Boston in New England, November 17, 1699" (*Memorial History of Boston*, 1881). The new church was called, by convention and for brevity's sake, the Manifesto Church.

The Manifesto Church with its slightly more liberal requirements for baptisms and church membership, was a departure in several ways from old-line Puritanism. Yet its members still held onto that streak of propriety we associate with Puritanism, as exemplified by their attitude toward music. When Thomas Brattle died in 1713 he willed the church an organ, which he had imported from England. It was the first of its kind in America. Though the organ was "dedicated and devoted to the praise and glory of God," the church voted that it was not proper for worship, and the gift was turned down (*Memorial History of Boston*, 1881). As specified in Brattle's will the organ was then offered to the King's Chapel on Tremont Street, where it was gladly accepted.

The Manifesto Church, like most congregational meetinghouses, was not designed to be a showplace. Constructed entirely of wood, it was never painted, inside or out. There were no clocks in the sanctuary, only a large hourglass that stood on the pulpit. Legend has it that the minister would begin his sermon after turning over the hourglass. Due to the nature of eighteenth-century preaching, many members of the congregation spent the sermon gazing longingly at the sand in the hourglass, waiting for it to empty. Unfortunately, once it finally did run out, the deacon would sometimes simply turn the hourglass over and continue his sermon.

Brattle Square, it should be noted, was also the original home of another religion in Boston. The first Quaker meeting house stood on the west side of the square from 1709 to 1729.

The Brattle Square Church, as the Manifesto Church came to be called, was soon embroiled in a perilous controversy. Because religion and medicine were barely distinguishable in Puritan Boston, the very lives of the townspeople hung in the balance. When a smallpox epidemic killed over a thousand people in the late 1600s, the clergy of Boston were united in their assessment of the cause: the sins of an errant flock had brought death to the town, and only a return to more basic theology could prevent the wrath of God from striking down even more people.

During the smallpox epidemic of 1720 to 1721, Dr. Zabdiel Boylston, who lived not far from the Brattle Square Church, advocated the inoculation of healthy people with small doses of smallpox as a way of building up their resistance to the disease. To a medically ignorant public this was something close to madness. They could not understand how contracting a mild form of a disease could prevent one from succumbing to a deadly form. In a surprising display of enlightenment, several members of Boston's ministry, among them Benjamin Colman of the Brattle Square Church, advocated the inoculation. Even Cotton Mather, the staunchly conservative leader of the Puritan Church in Boston, tried to persuade his flock. (For his stand Mather had a bomb thrown through a window of his home by one of the more ardent opponents of the inoculation plan.)

When the epidemic finally passed in 1722, the death totals proved Boylston's theory correct. Over one sixth of the population of Boston had perished from the disease, but only 6 of the 286 people who were inoculated had died. Inoculation soon became a standard form of health care in Boston, and Boylston was awarded a fellowship to the Royal Society of London.

The Brattle Square Church flourished. In 1772, when the members decided it was time to rebuild, Governor Bowdoin offered them the property he owned at the intersection of Tremont and Howard streets for the site of a new church. At

The Brattle Square Church, where many of the Revolution's leaders prayed, was used as a barrack by British troops quartered in Brattle Square during the Siege of Boston. The cannonball which struck the church the night before evacuation is visible to the right of the window just above the front door (Courtesy of the Bostonian Society/Old State House).

about the same time John Hancock offered the church a thousand pounds and a brand new bell for its steeple if the congregation remained in Brattle Square. Hancock was just one of the many leaders who prayed here, making this church highly influential during its time.

One can only speculate how differently Scollay Square would have turned out had the church taken Governor Bowdoin up on his offer; they would have ended up close to where the Howard Athenaeum would someday stand. The church took Hancock's offer, however, and on July 25, 1773, a new stone church was dedicated in Brattle Square. There, along with hosting many of the Revolution's leaders in prayer (among them Washington, Hancock, Adams, and Otis), the church would also have a role in the country's battle for independence.

Brattle Square During the Revolutionary War

Thanks to a series of taxes imposed on the American colonies by the British in the mid-1700s, resentment toward the British crown was growing. One of the centers of this discontent was Boston, where Samuel Adams, his cousin John, and others formed the Sons of Liberty. They met in many places, among them the Brattle Square home of the town clerk, William Cooper.

The "Circular Letter," written by Sam Adams and sent to the Parliament in England by the Massachusetts legislature in 1768, complained about new laws that had been imposed on the colonies and asserted the right of the colonists to govern themselves. This document enraged the British crown, which sent two regiments of the 29th infantry to Boston, where they were offered quarters in a sugar manufacturing house in Brattle Square owned by James Murray. A Scottish merchant with loyalist sympathies, Murray owned several buildings in Brattle Square.

The troops arrived in October 1768, led by General Thomas Gage. During his stay in Boston, Gage lived in Brattle Square in a home owned by Murray. His troops, also quartered in the square, practiced military exercises in front of the home of John Adams. One wonders how this tested the limits of both Revolutionary and family bonds, since John had just moved back to Boston from his home in Braintree at the urging of his cousin Sam. Now, because of Sam's oratory, John was subjected to the clatter of troops and equipment marching below his bedroom window.

John Adams is on record as being quite annoyed with the constant activity of the soldiers. So annoyed, in fact, that the following spring he moved to Portland Street, a block away. (Before moving away from Brattle Square, the future president lived in a home that he and his family called "The White House." This was the home of not one, but two future presidents, John and his one-year-old son, John Quincy Adams.)

For the most part, citizens of Boston tolerated the British encampment in Brattle Square, though there were reports of sporadic incidents between colonialists and British troops. These incidents climaxed two years later on March 5, 1770, when soldiers of the 29th infantry, facing an attacking mob, killed five colonists and wounded six others in what is known today as the Boston Massacre. (Ironically, the man who successfully defended the soldiers against a murder indictment was John Adams, no friend of the British but a man with a strong sense of justice.)

Three years later Parliament passed the Tea Act of 1773. The act removed all import duties on tea brought into England and allowed the East India Company to deal directly with American wholesalers. The Americans, instead of rejoicing over the lower cost of tea, were angered over what they felt was a loss of their freedom of choice.

So it was that on December 16, 1773, groups of men assembled at various places around Boston in preparation for a carefully planned display of protest. One such meeting was held at the Franklin Avenue office of Edes and Gill, printers. (Franklin Avenue, which still runs between Court Street and City Hall Plaza, was then a narrow lane only nine and a half feet wide, running from Court Street to a path that would in the next century become Cornhill.) That night they drank punch and disguised themselves as Indians before setting off for the Boston Tea Party, one of the most important events in Revolutionary War history.

Boston remained under British control for the next three years, during which time General Gage and his troops remained in Brattle Square. The Quartering Act was being used with little discretion by the British, who at one point attempted to take the Brattle Square Church and convert it into a riding school for the soldiers. The church, which had just been rebuilt in 1772, was a source of pride for Boston. The thought of tearing down the pillars so the soldiers would have room to ride inside the structure upset a lot of people, especially the deacon, Samuel Cooper. A fervent patriot and contributor to the revolutionary cause, Cooper had earned the nickname "Silver Tongue Sam." Living up to this reputation, he pointed out to the British that removing the supports would probably cause the building to collapse. This saved the church, which was used instead as a barrack. (Had it not been rebuilt in stone it might have suffered an even worse fate, as several churches made of wood were torn down and used for fuel by the British during the siege of Boston in 1775.)

During the siege the church did suffer one more indignity, when it was struck by cannon fire. Patriot artillery men on Lechmere point, located a mile or so away, were fond of testing the range of their guns by firing into British positions, including the main encampment in Brattle Square. In March 1776, on the night before the evacuation of British troops from Boston, a shell hit the Brattle Square Church just above the front door, dislodging some bits of stone and falling to the ground. It was picked up by a parishioner and stored in the rectory for many years until the church, possibly as part of the country's upcoming fiftieth anniversary celebration, placed it back in the wall in 1825. The shelling of the church was apparently held in great regard by Bostonians, and Oliver Holmes was later moved to write of the event in typically grandiose, nineteenth-century style. The church, he wrote:

> Wore on her bosom as a bride might do
> The iron breastpin the rebels threw.
> (*Historic Boston and Its Neighborhoods*, 1898)

Hanover Street

At the head of Hanover Street, which used to run through the North End from the harbor to the base of Beacon Hill in Scollay Square, stood the Concert Hall.

According to Samuel Adams Drake in his 1900 history of Boston, the hall became a place of great importance for many different people:

> The site was first known as Houchin's Corner, from a tanner of that name who occupied it. Concerts were held as early as January, 1755, when a "concert of musick" was advertised to take place there. Before the Revolution it was the resort of the Friends of Liberty, and as early as 1755, after the installation of Jeremy Gridley as Grand Master of the Masons in North America, it was used by the Grand Lodge for occasions of meeting or festivity, and continued to be so used until the present century. Here Captain Preston was dallying on the evening of the fatal March 1770, when he was summoned in hot haste to begin the first act of the great conflict of the American Revolution. The American prisoners captured at Bunker Hill are said to have been tried by a military court in Concert Hall (*Old Landmarks and Historic Personages of Boston*, 1900).

Across from the Concert Hall, on the north side of Hanover Street, was the Orange Tree Tavern, known for having the best well water in town — "never dry nor known to freeze," according to Drake. In 1712 the owner of the tavern, John Wardwell, set up what is believed to be the first hackney coach stand in Boston.

Hanover Street's most significant contribution comes not from having what amounts to the city's first taxi stand, however, but from the part that one of its residents played in what is undoubtedly the most famous horse ride in American history. Dr. Joseph Warren lived along the stretch of Hanover Street now buried between City Hall and the John F. Kennedy federal building. Warren, head of the Committee of Safety, was Boston's leading patriot. On April 16, 1775, he learned that British troops were preparing for action against the American weapon supply depots north of the city. His plan was to send two men to warn the colonists as soon as he knew which route the troops would take. When he learned, two days later, that the British were preparing to march on the stores in Lexington and Concord from the Boston Common, he sent for William Dawes and Paul Revere to spread the warning. And so it was, from this home on a street that would someday be part of Scollay Square, that the midnight ride of Paul Revere began.

George Washington Slept Here

After American independence, Scollay Square became the site of one of the first confrontations between men who advocated a strong national government and those who believed in state sovereignty, an issue that would one day propel the country into civil war.

In October 1789, the first president of the United States arrived in Boston. George Washington stayed at the home of Joseph Ingersoll, located on the south side of the intersection of Court and Tremont streets. (Today, across Court Street from the Steaming Kettle, the Hemenway Building now stands on this site.)

There to greet him was John Adams, who was vice president at the time. Governor of Massachusetts John Hancock had avoided the president's arrival as a way of displaying his staunch belief in the sovereignty of the state. After all, should not the president pay his respects to the governor of the state he was visiting? Washington was equally adamant in his belief that the governor should pay a call on the leader of the federal government. Hancock soon realized that he had made a diplomatic blunder. To the rescue came Lieutenant Governor Samuel Adams, who was anxious to avoid a confrontation so early in Washington's administration. That night, he paid the president a visit to explain that the governor had been ill.

Tears were said to have welled up in Washington's eyes when, the next day, Hancock, supposedly suffering from gout, was carried into the Ingersoll house by several servants. Some felt Hancock's illness was concocted to conceal bad judgment, but Washington was quick to drop the matter, and accept an invitation for tea.

CHAPTER 2

The Scollays and the Scollay Building

Some of the most frequently asked questions about Scollay Square (aside from the ones about Sally Keith's tassels), concern its origin. Just where did the name Scollay come from? What is known about the family who provided the name? Do any family members still live today, and if they do, what do they think of their family's namesake?

John Scollay was a member of the Sons of Liberty. His participation in the Revolution was overshadowed by that of the more prominent and outspoken revolutionaries such as Adams, Otis, and Hancock, but his contribution was nevertheless important. Without individuals like John Scollay supporting the cause, resisting the British might not have been possible.

Scollay came to Massachusetts from Scotland's Orkney Islands late in the seventeenth century. In 1692 he leased the Winnisimmet Ferry for one year and later took out a seven-year lease. He achieved a certain amount of stature in colonial Boston and was elected fire marshall in 1747, a position he held for thirty-five years.

In 1761, along with about fifty other men, Scollay signed a petition that was sent to King George III, protesting the illegal actions of the British revenue officers. A strong supporter of colonial claims against the empire, he was chosen to Boston's board of selectmen in 1764. The honor was repeated in 1773, and the following year he was made chairman, a title he held until 1790.

John Scollay had ten children, eight of them boys. The youngest, named William, was also active in the community, becoming clerk of the market in 1788 and selectman from 1792 to 1795. Following in his father's footsteps, he acted as fire marshall from 1792 to 1806. On August 20, 1792, he was named a colonel in the

Boston Regiment, a title he is said to have carried proudly. William Scollay's profession was listed in the town records as apothecary and druggist, occupations which he practiced from a store on Cornhill. But his biggest contribution to the city was in real estate.

During the latter part of the eighteenth century, William Scollay lived on Bussey Street near the home of Charles Bulfinch, Boston's most influential architect of the time. They became friends and soon were involved in a joint real estate venture. Along with several other businessmen, they built the first block of buildings in Boston. Located on what is today Franklin Place, this curving row of buildings, designed by Bulfinch, was to be financed under a tontine plan, which led the developers to name it Tontine Crescent. According to the rules of the plan, the last surviving member of the original group of investors would own the entire property. Problems with construction caused members to abandon the tontine aspect of the project, although the Crescent was eventually built. (Today Franklin Place still follows the original curve of Bulfinch's plans.)

The Scollay Building

In the middle of Court Street, at the intersection of Court and Tremont, were a series of buildings which extended down Court Street to the head of Hanover Street. Nearest the intersection was a two-story brick building. The rest of the property, which narrowed as it extended west toward Hanover Street, was covered with wooden structures one or two stories high. Here one of the oldest printing houses in Boston, Green & Russell, transacted business around 1755. Part of this property also included some land at the base of Beacon Hill, on which stood a three-story mansion.

Russell, who had become owner of the property in the 1760s, sold it to William Vassall for three hundred pounds in 1774. Vassall moved into the mansion where he lived for two years. Then, following the British evacuation of Boston, the loyalist was forced to make a hasty retreat of his own. Patrick Jeffrey, a real estate investor, was able to buy the property for a little more than half of what Vassall had paid, about one hundred and sixty pounds.

The source of Jeffrey's money deserves some discussion, as it was the cause of some titters among Boston society around the time of the Revolution. A woman named Mary Wilkes Haley had arrived in Boston to inspect the property of her deceased husband, Alderman Haley. When this seventy-year-old woman married the thirty-year-old Jeffrey (who was in charge of the estate), Boston was both shocked and amused. No one was surprised, however, when the marriage broke up and Mrs. Haley returned to England. Jeffrey, now quite well off, was able to make purchases such as the Vassall estate.

In 1795 Jeffrey sold the Court Street property (which included the buildings in the middle of the street) to Colonel William Scollay. Jeffrey kept the Beacon Hill

The Scollay Building as it appeared just after the Civil War. The trolley tracks on either side of the building give little hint of the enormous impact that trolleys were having on the Square (Courtesy of the Bostonian Society/Old State House).

estate for a few more years, eventually selling it to Gardiner Greene. (There will be more about Greene and his property later.) Scollay moved into the brick building nearest Tremont Street and rented out the others. He named his new home on Court Street Scollay's Building, although the name also came to apply collectively to the other, smaller wooden structures on the property as well.

Considering the infamy the soon-to-be constructed Athenaeum on Howard Street would have, it is interesting to learn that the more intellectually oriented Boston Athenaeum (which now resides on Beacon Hill) was located in Scollay's Building from 1807 to 1809. The Provident Institution for Savings had its first branch here from 1823 to 1832. The building was also a popular location for lawyers since it was so close to the Court House, which had been built nearby on Court Street (near the old State House) in 1810.

The grade of Court Street was so steep at this time that someone walking on the Beacon Hill side of the street could see over the lower buildings on Scollay's property to the other side. When Court Street was leveled, Scollay's building gained a basement. There, a popular barber of the early 1800s named Bob New practiced his trade with great success, and Boston's best tea shop, its largest thread store, and a toy store all did business.

William Scollay had willed the buildings to his heirs and upon his death in 1809 they leased the property to a Mr. Dimmock. After having the two-story brick building inspected by two engineers, who pronounced the foundation safe, Dimmock had two more stories added, making the structure four stories tall. Scollay's Building, then one of the tallest in Boston, became the centerpiece for this part of town which, thanks to a growing transportation system, would evolve into a bustling commercial center.

How Scollay Square Got Its Name

Public transportation in Boston after Independence consisted mostly of stage lines that ran to and from the "suburbs." Because the Square was centrally located near the docks, Beacon Hill, and downtown, the intersection of Court and Tremont streets became a transfer point for early nineteenth-century commuters.

The Charlestown line ran every seven minutes and ended its run in front of the brick building owned by the Scollays. So did the Dorchester, Malden, and Cambridge coaches. Since there was no official designation for the stop, conductors merely used the name of the building to indicate where the trolley had stopped. Travelers on these lines would often tell their friends to meet them at Scollay's Building, and after a while the area became known as Scollay's Square. In 1838 the popular designation became official.

Ironically, improvements to Scollay Square, combined with increased traffic congestion, did more to threaten the existence of Scollay's buildings than to enhance their profitability. The traffic that had given rise to the name Scollay Square became the reason that some people wanted to tear the buildings down. Large stagecoaches and omnibuses, some of them led by four- and six-horse teams, were having trouble making the turn from Brattle Street onto Court Street. In 1841 a group of citizens unsuccessfully attempted to appropriate $10,000 to buy the buildings and have them removed. By the 1850s, thanks to their age and general disrepair, all the original wooden buildings had been torn down, leaving the four-story stone Scollay's Building to stand alone in the Square.

Traffic jams had long plagued Scollay Square. In 1784 the town was petitioned to widen Court Street near the old Concert Hall at Hanover Street. The petition read, in part:

> It is still so narrow that two carts cannot pass with safety — and as there are several shops opposite belonging to the town, much out of repair, the town is asked to widen at this point which will make the shops more convenient and fetch equal rent (*The Scollays*, 1906).

The petition was not granted, although public pressure forced the city to widen Court Street between Sudbury Street and Bowdoin Square in 1807. (Future traffic woes would later create the need for electric trolleys, and eventually America's first subway, in Scollay Square.)

On January 7, 1868, the Scollay family ended its association with Scollay's Building when they sold it and the property on Court Street to Arioch Wentworth for $100,000. Three years later Wentworth sold the building to the city for twice what he had paid the Scollays. That year, the city finally granted the wishes of many traffic-weary citizens when it tore Scollay's Building down, leaving the Square completely open.

The removal of Scollay's Building created a problem for topographers. "The open space is known as Scollay Square, although it is in fact the most irregular of triangles," Winsor Justin wrote soon after the building was torn down. "Two of the sides, and those two which form almost a right angle with each other, are in Court Street, and the third is Tremont Row. The removal of the buildings has left one of the most remarkable cases of confusion in street nomenclature anywhere to be found" (*Memorial History of Boston*, 1881).

Despite the intellectual confusion, there was no attempt to rename the intersection, and Scollay Square remained, at least in name.

The Scollay Family

Of John Scollay's other children, two have stories worth mentioning. One of his daughters married Colonel Thomas Melville, a participant in the Boston Tea

Party. The morning after the Tea Party she found tea leaves in the shoes he had worn the night before, but maintained her silence once she realized her husband's life was in jeopardy. She did save the tea leaves, however, which were preserved and later given to a local historical society.

Another daughter, Mercy Scollay, was a close friend of Benedict Arnold. He had taken an interest in the children of the late General Warren, who were under her care, and was attempting to raise money from the new government to support their education. In correspondence with Mercy he wrote that if Congress did not oblige he would provide whatever money was needed to raise the children. (Perhaps his plea for funds would have been successful if he hadn't changed sides before the war ended.)

William Scollay was the only son to reach manhood, and none of his sons lived to have a family. There are people today, however, who can trace their heritage back to the Scollays of Boston. In 1987, while working to have Government Center renamed Scollay Square, radio talk show host Jerry Williams received this letter:

> I am a direct descendent of the Scollay who gave the square its name.
> While the surname "Scollay" rarely appeared after the death of William Scollay, one lineage has been carried on through his daughter Lucy C. Scollay who married Benjeman Whitwell. Their daughter, Lucy Cushing Whitwell married William Parker. Their son, William Whitwell Parker married Harriet Esther Bell. Their son, William Bell Parker married Helen Sutliff. I am their son, Scollay Cortlandt Parker. Consequently I am in the fifth generation of that lineage (Scollay Parker to Jerry Williams, January 4, 1987).

Fred Scollay, a television actor, is also a direct descendant of John Scollay, although while being interviewed by Williams he said that he prefers to say his name with a slight French accent "to keep people from misspelling and mispronouncing it!" That's undoubtedly a good idea, since many people, even those who claim to be Scollay Square experts (myself included), constantly say "Scully."

To the Scollays we owe more than just thanks for giving the Square its name. Both John and his son William were civic-minded men who risked everything in their pursuit of American Independence. Today, if you visit the Massachusetts State House, you will see inscribed on the cornerstone, along with other, more familiar names from the Revolution, the name of William Scollay.

From Top Hats

to Footlights

The Square Grows Up

Following the Revolution, Boston was a seaport town of approximately eighteen thousand people engaged mostly in trade and manufacture. The great Back Bay landfill project of the nineteenth century was several decades away from consideration, meaning that most of Boston's citizens still lived and worked on the original isthmus founded by Winthrop almost two hundred years before. Scollay Square, thanks to the stagecoach and trolley activity, was at its very heart.

Despite the bustle and commotion caused by its location, Scollay Square still managed, during the first few decades of the 1800s, an erudite air. There were at this time no theaters, tattoo parlors, or hot dog stands in which to while away the time. The Square was far enough away from the docks to be considered residential, and some of Boston's most prominent citizens lived in and around the area. This easy mix of small businesses, churches, banks, and mansion homes would last for the first third of the century, until developers began the process that changed both Scollay Square and Boston.

Pemberton Square and Tremont Row

Directly across the street from Scollay's Building, on what was originally the site of Reverand John Cotton's home at the base of Beacon Hill, stood the Gardiner Greene Estate. Greene was a rich Demerara planter, who had married the daughter of Boston painter John Singleton Copley. Greene had purchased the property, on which stood a three-story mansion, from Patrick Jeffrey in 1803.

Greene developed the grounds of his estate into a magnificent terraced garden that was the pride of Boston. Spreading up Pemberton Hill (formerly Cotton Hill, renamed in the mid-1700s for the resident James Pemberton), with imported shrubbery, trees, peacocks, grapevines, and several greenhouses, the property ended nearly seventy feet above the current height of Pemberton Square. The estate had one of the finest views of Boston and the harbor. It was said that Nahant, a seashore town about fifteen miles away, was visible on clear days. Daniel Webster lived not far from the gardens and, according to Walter Muir Whitehill, was fond of climbing the hill to enjoy what he called a "magnificent panorama" (*Boston: A Topographical History*, 1968).

This bucolic serenity would not last, however, because Pemberton Hill was about to undergo a drastic change, thanks to the vision of Patrick Tracy Jackson. Among the most successful businessmen of the early nineteenth century, he was a man who truly deserves the title of entrepreneur. Long before there was any "Massachusetts Miracle," Jackson was creating some economic miracles of his own. As a founder of the textile mills in Lowell and treasurer of the Boston and Lowell Railroad, Jackson was already one of the most influential businessmen in Boston. His latest scheme would make him one the city's leading real estate developers.

After Gardiner Greene's death in 1832, Jackson purchased his property, but not because he was a garden lover. His plan was to cut off approximately seventy feet of Pemberton Hill and have the dirt used as landfill in the West End of Boston near what is today North Station. The remaining lot above Scollay Square would be subdivided and sold to prospective home builders. It was a plan worthy of the city that would soon double its land area by filling in the Back Bay.

In 1835 Jackson hired Asa Sheldon, a Wilmington farmer, to supervise the job. Sheldon, in turn, hired more than two hundred and fifty men who worked for exactly five months on the demolition of the hill. The entire project cost thirty thousand dollars, which, after expenses, netted farmer Sheldon a tidy one thousand seven hundred dollars. (The next year Sheldon completed the job when he filled in the marsh near North Station and created Lowell, Nashua, Haverhill, Andover, and Billerica streets using the land taken from Pemberton Hill.)

On October 5, 1835, just one day after the last cart of dirt was hauled away from Pemberton Hill, lots were sold at auction. To maintain architectural integrity, homes were subject to restrictions on height and design. For the next two decades the newly created Pemberton Square maintained a charming residential atmosphere. Its location just below Beacon Hill helped make it a popular address for the rich. The Lowells, Winthrops, Forbeses, Cabots, Coolidges, and Crowinshields were just some of the residents of what was first called Phillips Place. By 1838, when the name was changed to Pemberton Square, it was the undisputed center of Boston aristocracy, where at one point almost half of the millionaires in New England lived. This was to change, however, as Scollay Square below began

Pemberton Square, 1860 (Courtesy of the Bostonian Society/Old State House).

Pemberton Square, 1934. The courthouse replaced the west side of the square in 1886. Most of the original bow-front homes had already given way to offices and apartment buildings by that time; the rest were gone by the end of the century (Courtesy of the Bostonian Society/Old State House).

Pemberton Square, 1989. Across from the courthouse is the rear of One Two Three Center Plaza (Author's collection).

to reflect the enormous geographical and social transformations taking place in Boston.

When Patrick Tracy Jackson removed the Greene estate he not only created Pemberton Square but also provided for a row of buildings on Court Street in Scollay Square. As in Pemberton Square, they were built to certain architectural specifications, though these buildings would be for businesses, not homes. The development was called Tremont Row. An eclectic mix of shops, law offices, and small businesses, Tremont Row catered to the class of people who could afford to live in nearby Pemberton Square.

For example, at number 21 Tremont Row was the Lorenzo Papanti Dance Academy. It was the kind of establishment that helped give Scollay Square its aristocratic air, thanks to the giant ballroom to which Boston's elite flocked for various social events. Here in Scollay Square, America first danced the waltz. It was at Papanti's, in 1842, that Boston was introduced to Charles Dickens, who by that time had written the immensely popular *Pickwick Papers* and *Oliver Twist*.

Next door, at number 19 Tremont Row, two of the first photographers and daguerreotypists in Boston set up shop. These were new and expensive pursuits, but the studios of Southworth and Hawes were well situated near people who could afford the luxury of having their portraits taken. Above the Hawes studio, a dental surgery technique was introduced. Dr. William Thomas Morton and Dr. Harold Wells advertised dental services "under their new improved method," the

The Gardiner Greene estate, around the beginning of the nineteenth century. Behind this home, Cotton Hill rose over seventy feet. Its exquisite garden was a major tourist attraction in Boston (Courtesy of the Bostonian Society/Old State House).

Tremont Row, during the mid nineteenth century, when it was home to the Papanti Dance Studio, Dr. Morton, and J.J. Hawes (Courtesy of the Bostonian Society/Old State House).

One Two Three Center Plaza, which replaced Tremont Row. Kings Chapel and the Parker House (down Tremont Street) are visible on the far left (Author's collection).

use of anesthesia. From Dr. Morton's and Mr. Hawes's time right up until demolition (as many visitors to Scollay Square will tell you), the area never suffered for the lack of photography studios or painless dentists.

The Modern Era Begins

Two massive changes occurred in Boston during the 1800s. One was sociological and the other was topographical. By the time the transition was complete, Tremont Row and the rest of Scollay Square had gone through two transformations. The first solidified the Square's place as a transportation and commercial center, while the second made it Boston's entertainment mecca.

Tremendous numbers of Irish escaping the great potato famine of the 1840s emigrated to Boston and took up residence in the city, many in the North End and some in the West End, both areas located just outside Scollay Square. It was this great flood of immigration that began the transformation of Boston from a Yankee-dominated town to a genuine melting pot.

As Boston laid more and more trolley track it became easier for those who could not afford private transportation to move around the city. Scollay Square was, by virtue of its location, already a center of transportation. The influx of Irish and the trolley traffic now caused the first change in the character of the Square. No longer an erudite collection of upper-class business, it was quickly developing into a shopping center that catered to travelers, commuters, and immigrants.

Friction between the Irish-Catholic immigrants and the established Yankee-Protestants was immediate, so when the Back Bay fill-in project (begun in 1859) created new property west of the Public Garden, many of those who could afford to move did so with little hesitation. As the elite moved farther away from Scollay Square, the businesses left behind had a choice: either adapt to the new working-class clientele or close. Fine hotels like the American House, the Quincy House (Boston's first building made from Quincy granite), and Young's Hotel became more like boardinghouses than the fine hostelries they were originally intended to be. Elegant restaurants became cafeterias. Haberdashers who once carried silk top hats now sold woolen scully caps. Dance academies became tap dance studios. And around the corner from Tremont Row on Howard Street, the Howard Athenaeum, which during the 1850s presented William MacReady, the greatest Shakespearean actor of the day, twenty years later touted minstrel shows and seats in the gallery for just fifteen cents.

But it wasn't just businesses that felt the impact of Boston's westward movement. The Brattle Square Church was a year shy of its one hundredth birthday when it was torn down in 1871, mostly due to a shortage of parishioners. The congregation, like many of its neighbors, had moved to the Back Bay. Leopold Morse and Company, clothiers, bought the property, tore the church down, and erected a large store on the site.

Meanwhile, as Scollay Square changed to serve the public with more popular venues, Pemberton Square was experiencing its own transformation. As the rich moved farther up Beacon Hill to get away from the increasing din of Scollay Square, some of the homes that were once single family residences were turned into boardinghouses. With the courthouse and Boston City Hall located a short distance away down Court Street and the Massachusetts state capitol just up Beacon Hill, many lawyers found Pemberton Square the perfect location from which to practice, and so several homes were purchased and converted into offices. Eventually most of these residences were torn down and replaced by large office buildings that could handle the increasing numbers of lawyers who, by the 1880s, practiced in Pemberton Square.

In 1886 construction was begun on a new courthouse in Pemberton Square, and soon after that the headquarters for the Boston police department was completed there. At about the same time, Boston University's executive building, Jacob Sleeper Hall, was constructed at the square's rear entrance. Once shielded from the hustle and bustle of the world, Pemberton Square had, by the late 1800s, joined Scollay Square in the center of it all.

The Heyday of Scollay Square

By the late 1870s Scollay Square's first transformation was complete. It was now a thriving part of Boston's wholesale business district. At this time, except for the Howard Athenaeum, most businesses were geared toward sales and merchandising, not entertainment. But the Scollay Square that most Bostonians remember was one filled with theatres, arcades, bars, nightclubs, and amusement centers. It was a place geared almost solely for amusement.

Credit for this next transformation must first be given to the Howard Athenaeum, which, as we shall see in the next chapter, had turned to popular entertainment after the Civil War. This opened up a whole new avenue for businesses in Scollay Square, many of which became hotels and restaurants catering to actors and theatergoers. The streets surrounding the Howard began to take on a character all their own. Fred Allen wrote about this area in his autobiography:

> There were many places to eat and things to do. On Howard Street was Higgen's Famous Oyster House. The Higgens enterprise consisted of five small buildings joined together, merging into a hotel, a bar, the Cafe Oriental Room, and the famous glassed-in Palm Garden. The oysters must have had something to do with the hotel's success.
>
> There were thirty-five rooms in the hotel, and many days five hundred were rented. Bellboys at the Higgens averaged fifty dollars a day. The Higgens slogan was "Your grandfather dined here." The slogan didn't mention what else your grandfather might have done there (*Much Ado About Me*, 1956).

Other restaurants and bars included the Daisy Lunch, located next to the Howard theater, the Grotto, and Jack's Cafe. Since much of the clientele were actors, sailors, and Boston residents looking for a cheap night out, the price of a meal at most of these establishments was usually inexpensive.

Aside from the restaurants, there were numerous rooming houses and hotels for actors. The William Tell Hotel was located on Howard Street. Rent was five dollars a week, including meals. Nonguests who wished to eat there paid a quarter for a full course meal in 1912. The most famous of the actors' hotels was the Rexford, also on Howard Street. Most of the women who toured with the burlesque shows stayed at the Rexford, which made it very popular with the actors, even if they weren't staying there themselves.

The nearby Revere House in Bowdoin Square at one time played host to Presidents Fillmore, Pierce, Johnson, and Grant; the Grand Duke Alexis of Russia; Emperor Dom Pedro II of Brazil; and, in 1860, the future Edward VII, who at that time was the Prince of Wales. From its opening in 1846 until after the Civil War, the Revere House was regarded as one of Boston's finest hotels. But by the early 1900s it was hard to find people who remembered when it was anything but just another hotel, although the restaurant was still highly recommended.

The other ingredient in Scollay Square's evolution was the sailor. Since its earliest days, Boston thrived as a seaport. Seaports need sailors, and sailors need something to do on shore leave. This was as true in the late 1800s as it was in the early 1600s. The Charlestown shipyards, located across Boston Harbor and just minutes from Scollay Square by trolley, deposited throngs of lonely, entertainment-starved swabbies along its streets (drawn, in no small part, by the Old Howard), thus helping to explain the many tattoo parlors, bars, and rent-by-the-hour hotels that began to appear.

The Theaters

Thanks to the Old Howard and the sailors, Boston's Puritan aversion to the theater was supplanted by a stronger desire for diversion. Tremont Row, around the

MEET ME AT THE
NEW PALACE THEATRE
COURT, SUDBURY AND SCOLLAY SQ.
A SWELL SHOW
Continuous 10 A. M. till 11 P. M.

It was in the attic of 109 Court Street (home, at the turn of the century, to the Palace Theatre) that Thomas Edison produced his first patented invention and several years later Alexander Graham Bell and Thomas Watson first heard the sound of a human voice through a telephone. The workshop where Bell and Watson achieved this feat was dismantled under Watson's supervision and is on display today at the phone company building in downtown Boston (Courtesy of Fred McLellan).

The Theatre Comique was the first theater in Boston built expressly for showing motion pictures (Courtesy of the Bostonian Society/Old State House).

The Star Theatre and Austin & Stones in 1911. The Star had a unique air conditioning system: large blocks of ice were placed in a trough, covered by metal grating, which ran along the center of the aisle (Courtesy of the Bostonian Society/Old State House).

Scollay's Olympia, which replaced Austin & Stones in 1912, was one of the first buildings erected in Boston using steel reinforced concrete (Courtesy of the Bostonian Society/Old State House).

corner from the popular Howard theater and just a stone's throw from many restaurants and eateries, provided the ideal location for places of this sort. One such
establishment belonged to none other than Phineas T. Barnum. For thirty years
(beginning in 1881), his Austin & Stones Dime Museum, located at the corner of
Howard Street and Tremont Row, presented a mix of vaudeville acts (among them
Weber and Fields), and carnival freaks. It was a far cry from the Papanti Dance
Academy.

The master of ceremonies at Austin & Ştones was the loquacious Professor William S. Hutchings, formerly with the Barnum & Bailey circus, where he was
known as the Boy Lightning Calculator. At Austin & Stones he was a cross between carnival barker and lecturer. "The professor's mouth was an adjective hutch,
and . . . was loath to use one word when eight or nine would do," says Fred Allen. As he finished introducing each exhibit to the crowd, the professor would ac-
centuate the end of his sentence with the words "Marvelous! Marvelous!" (*Much
Ado About Me*, 1956). It was said that Harvard students who studied speech and
forensics were urged by their teachers to listen to the professor at work. They
never went away disappointed.

From his stage the professor introduced the Ossified Man, whose condition
"was caused by an overdeveloped case of arthritis and would eventually cause him
one day to become his own tombstone." There was also Riley, the Man-Fish; Jo-Jo
the Dog Faced Boy; Eko and Iko, two albinos; Howard the Lobster Boy, "whose
both hands and feet are lobster claws"; and Mlle. Airline, the Human Match, "who
contains so much vital fire that she can light a gas jet by touching it with only the
tips of her fingers" (*Much Ado About Me*, 1956).

When the professor died in 1911, so did Austin & Stones. It seemed that as many
people went to hear the professor as to see the freaks. The following year it was
torn down to make way for a new vaudeville theater, Scollay's Olympia. Completed in 1912, the Olympia had the distinction of being the first building in Boston constructed with steel-reinforced concrete. The Olympia was one of the places
where vaudevillians such as Milton Berle began their careers. Berle, who used to
do a blackface routine, once remarked that the box seats were so close to the stage
"that I always felt I might be attacked when a joke bombed" (*Boston Herald*, April
30, 1987).

Though movies had been marketed for several years, they were so jittery and
uneven that it was impossible to watch them for any length of time. Most theater
owners, like the Olympia's, were unimpressed with the technology, choosing instead a live stage. But others found great success in the new entertainment.

For instance, the Theatre Comique was the first theater in Boston built speci-
fically for showing films when it opened in 1906 near Tremont Row. The price
for the half-hour show was ten cents, and the theater, which held about 350 seats,
was often filled to capacity during the first few years it was open. A typical program consisted of a movie and several "illustrated songs," precursors to the "follow
the bouncing ball" sing-alongs of later years.

The Star, which opened at about the same time and was located next door to Austin & Stones, held about 365 seats. Manager T. Campbell, who had a movie screen and projector installed, wrote:

> During the first year and a half that I managed this theatre, very often we used to open at nine in the morning to a capacity house and run shows as short as twelve minutes duration, after which we would pass people out through a rear exit and there would be more than enough people waiting to fill the house again. This would continue until we closed at eleven o'clock at night (*Fifty Years of Boston*, 1932).

As movie technology improved and became less of a burden on a person's eyesight, the length of the features increased. According to Campbell:

> All of our shows in those days used to run a full week; that is, we would rent about three reels for a full week and would show any part of the same according to the amount of business done. The shows naturally ran from a minimum of twelve minutes to a maximum of about forty-five minutes. As more theatres opened, the shows commenced to increase in length, until at last we were presenting shows of an hour's duration (*Fifty Years of Boston*, 1932).

The nearby Palace and Beacon theaters at first featured live talent such as local boys "Sliding" Billy Watson (named for his across-the-stage skid on a banana peel) and Dave Marion. Movie screens were later installed as an additional novelty. Soon, the live shows disappeared and the theaters became strictly moviehouses.

Though the theaters helped bring thousands of people from all over the metropolitan area to Scollay Square, the Star, Palace, Bowdoin, and Olympia were considered neighborhood theaters by most West Enders:

> The Bowdoin used to have local talent shows. It was just like you see in the old movies. If the audience didn't like somebody they had this big hook, which would come out from the side of the stage and pull them off. I won a dollar for singing "Rosie O'Grady" one night. I couldn't keep it, of course. I had to give it to my family.

Joe, another West Ender, remembered:

> When we were kids and poor, one of the things we used to do was go into Scollay Square and look at the lights on the theaters. The one I remember best was the Star because they had this star made of lights and it would rotate.

As popular as the sailors and other adults made the Square at night, it was the children who packed the theaters during the day:

> We used to pay ten cents to get into the Olympia and we used to watch the movie while the piano played the soundtrack. We used to then stand on the corner of Howard Street and watch the bald-headed men go into the Old Howard. That was

the biggest thrill. You could go into two or three theaters and see a movie and a live show. Candy was five cents a bag and when the action got exciting the piano would play faster and when there was a love scene the piano would play slow. We kids loved it. It was fantastic. We used to go on a Saturday, after spending the morning doing chores at our West End homes and get a reward to go to the movies in the afternoon (Bob W.).

The Scollay Square Theatre on Saturday mornings would have a program for kids. I'd sit through three shows just to see what happened. They had Pearl White tied to the tracks and she was about to be squashed by a train. I would stay to see if she really got squashed but it would always end in the same place (Gladys Shapiro).

Like Bob and Gladys, many people brought up before and during the Depression remember Saturday excursions into the city with a bag lunch and ten cents in their pocket. When the subway stopped at Scollay Square they would head for one of the theaters on Tremont Row such as Scollay's Olympia or the Star. Another former West Ender mused, "It was a good place to get rid of the kids for a day. Mothers used to give their kids lunch and leave them there for the day."

Their parents would then depart for Washington Street and the stores downtown while the kids enjoyed *The Perils of Pauline* or *William Farnum*. Crowded two or three to a seat, they were kept in line by a policeman who walked the aisles and would rap the end of the row with his billy club if they got too noisy. "I could still feel the seats reverberating minutes after he passed," one former moviegoer said. "I can still feel them now."

By the 1910s, the evolution of Scollay Square was complete. The Old Howard was pure burlesque, and every sailor who got liberty in Boston was making it a point to visit the Square. What the Brahmins and the Yankees had abandoned, others were quick to make their own. Fred Allen said it best:

If the Boston of those days was as proper and conservative as the high-button shoe, the average man's answer to conservatism was Scollay Square. Scollay Square was the hot foot applied to the high-button shoe (*Much Ado About Me*, 1956).

It was during this period of incredible growth and transformation that Scollay Square began to acquire its legendary status. It is not yet the era of Sally Keith and her tassels, but one of giant tea kettles, mobile statues, abolitionists, cavalry charges, and three of the country's greatest contributors to modern electronics.

Cornhill

Describing for newcomers to Boston just where all the streets of Scollay Square were located can be a daunting task. So much was torn down and paved over in the early 1960s that almost nothing remains from the time when the Square was alive.

Thankfully the developers saved one small piece. On the south side of City Hall Plaza, there is a curved, red building with a giant tea kettle hanging above a first-floor door. This is the Sears Crescent Building, which today clearly defines the path that Cornhill took when that road was first laid out in 1816 by developer Uriah Cotting. Cotting's aim was to create a graceful entrance to Faneuil Hall and the Dock Square area from Beacon Hill. By statute, the buildings had to be designed according to certain specifications laid out by the developer, ensuring the architectural harmony of the street.

It was first named Cheapside, the British word for a market. A year later the name was changed to use the American vernacular, Market Street. In 1829 the name Market Street was given to a street near Faneuil Hall, and the name Cornhill, which had been the name of Washington Street until 1824, was revived and given to Cotting's creation. (The name, by the way, was simply Cornhill. To append Cornhill with the word *street* or *avenue* is a Boston faux pas not unlike adding an *s* to the word Common.)

The Sears Crescent Building, named for Yankee merchant and developer David Sears, who purchased the property just before his death, was constructed in 1841. Originally four stories high, it was amended in 1848 with the prow that still stretches along the top. It was in the next century, according to John Harris, that "No less a national figure than Speaker Thomas P. "Tip" O'Neill, Jr., standing upstairs at an open window in the prow of the Sears block, could be seen during a campaign addressing throngs in the square below" (*Historic Walks in Old Boston*, 1982).

Cornhill enjoyed a glorious history as the center for used and antique books in Boston. For over one hundred years, starting in the mid-1800s, there were, on the average, thirty bookstores on Cornhill catering to people from all walks of life. Students such as Harvard undergrads Franklin D. Roosevelt and John F. Kennedy were constantly prowling the stacks in search of rare books and research material. During Boston's notorious period of book banning in the 1920s and 1930s, Cornhill became a symbol of literary oppression when it was, according to Jane Holtz Kay, reduced to "four dusty tunnels" (*Lost Boston*, 1980).

Selling books and magazines wasn't the only literary occupation on Cornhill, however. Many publishing houses had their presses there too, as did newspaper and pamphlet publishers. And some of them managed to do more than report the news; they actually *made* the news.

In 1831 a young abolitionist newspaper publisher named William Lloyd Garrison moved his presses to 25 Cornhill. Garrison's work was extremely controversial, and twice he was dragged from his Cornhill office through the streets of Boston by angry mobs who tarred and feathered him. He was evicted several times by nervous landlords and eventually moved to 37 Cornhill, where he was joined at times by Thoreau, Emerson, Hawthorne, and Whittier, men who made this part of Cornhill the center of Boston's antislavery movement. It was in the Garrison offices that Harriet Beecher Stowe wrote *Uncle Tom's Cabin* and where Julia Ward Howe began "The Battle Hymn of the Republic," the song that became synonymous with the Civil War.

During the Civil War, hundreds of runaway slaves were hidden in the basement of Garrison's Cornhill office, which served as a vital link in the famous Underground Railroad. Countless lives were saved by Garrison and his fellow Abolitionists in Scollay Square. Though the intellectual intensity of that era did not last much past the Civil War, the bookstores remained an integral part of Cornhill right up until the very last days of Scollay Square.

Morse

At the head of Brattle Street was the home of John Smibert, America's first professional portraitist. He was considered by some to be the foremost painter in America at the time. One of his most famous portraits was of his good friend Peter Faneuil, who had Smibert design the original Faneuil Hall in 1742. John Trumbell, who is best known for his painting of *The Battle of Bunker Hill* (which sits in the rotunda of the Capitol building in Washington, D.C.), studied in Smibert's studio after resigning his commission in the Revolutionary Army in 1777.

The Smibert studio was taken over by painter Washington Allston in 1809. It was here that young Samuel F. B. Morse, the inventor of the electric telegraph, studied art while attending Yale University. Like many college art students, Morse worked his way through school by painting portraits: five dollars for miniatures and one dollar for profiles. Before work on telegraphy took over his life, Morse painted the portraits of the Marquis de Lafayette and Eli Whitney.

Interestingly, it was applications of Morse's telegraphy that years later brought both Thomas Alva Edison and Alexander Graham Bell to Boston and Scollay Square.

Edison

Thomas Edison was a twenty-one-year-old drifter with a skill for telegraphy when he arrived in Boston in March 1868. A dazzling display of Morse code reading ability earned him a job with the local Western Union office after being in the city for just a few hours.

He worked alongside young men who were either attending, or had just graduated from, some of the most prestigious colleges in America, among them Harvard and Columbia. Edison once remarked how these young scholars constantly paraded their knowledge in front of him, knowing that the extent of his education was not even high school level.

To compensate, Edison went to the secondhand bookstores along Cornhill and sought questions he could spring on them during conversation. It was here that he found a set of Michael Faraday's two-volume *Experimental Researches in Electricity*. Edison would someday light entire cities with electricity, and it was among the book stacks on Cornhill that the young inventor first imagined the power of the dynamo. He described his excitement at the find:

> [Faraday's] explanations were simple. He used no mathematics. He was the master experimenter. I don't think there were many copies of Faraday's works sold in those days. The only people who did anything in electricity were the telegraphers and the opticians making simple school apparatus to demonstrate the principles (*Light for the World*, 1967).

During the evening Edison worked at the Western Union office and by day he collected books and electrical equipment to duplicate Faraday's experiments. He became friends with a man named Charles Williams, another inventor and experimenter, who owned a small shop at 109 Court Street. The shop had been in business for almost twenty years, making all sorts of electrical devices, such as fire alarms, bells, gongs, batteries, telegraph apparatus, and an assortment of custom-made gadgets for inventors and scientists. Robert V. Bruce, in his biography of Alexander Graham Bell, described Williams's shop this way:

> In the main shop, dust and soot had long since turned the whitewashed brick walls into a streaked and shadowy gray. Near the grimy front and back windows stood a dozen or more metalworking hand lathes and a couple of small steam powered lathes. Under dusty ceiling beams, pulleys whirred and quivered leather belts raced along their endless courses. Wooden racks of steel, iron and brass sheets and rods huddled in the center, and piles of rough castings lay about the floor. A small forge for annealing and tempering joined the steam engine in adding heat to the noise, dust and movement of the place (*Alexander Bell and the Conquest of Solitude*, 1973).

Williams gave Edison a small corner of the shop where he worked on various projects in his spare time. Here in Scollay Square, Thomas Edison began a remarkable career with his first patented invention, an automatic vote-counter. The patent was granted in mid-1869. Edison went to Washington to display his invention before a committee of Congressmen, certain his invention would be welcomed there and in every legislative body in the country. He was wrong. It seemed that lawmakers used the lumbering voice-vote as a way of stalling unwanted legislation. His device would ruin the time-honored tradition of filibustering and it was turned down. Edison returned to Boston vowing never again to invent anything he could not sell.

Edison's Scollay Square work produced two more inventions. One was a device to allow two-way use of a single telegraph wire, called a duplex (or multiple) telegraph. That invention failed its first public demonstration and was abandoned. The other was a stock ticker, which he successfully demonstrated and sold to several subscribers. Unfortunately, Edison was so wrapped up in the technical details of the stock ticker that the investors were able to take his invention away from him. By mid-1869, Edison, as broke as he was when he first arrived, decided his reputation in Boston would keep any new investors from making cash available for his experiments, so he set off for New York, leaving Scollay Square (and all of his equipment) behind.

Bell

A man named Thomas Watson worked in the Williams shop for many years. One day, in 1879, Watson was working on an electrical device when the man who had ordered it showed up to request some changes to the original plans. The two men hit it off almost immediately, the inventor impressed by Watson's fine technical abilities and Watson in turn awed by the inventor's manners and command of the language. Soon Watson was working exclusively for Alexander Graham Bell.

Bell, who was teaching the deaf and lecturing at Boston University to earn money for his experiments, was attempting to develop one of the things that had eluded Edison several years back in the same shop, a multiple telegraph. For Bell, however, it was a means to reach his goal of transmitting the human voice electrically over wire. In June 1875, Bell and Watson successfully tested the duplex telegraph, an important first step on the road to the telephone.

On July 1, 1875, Alexander Graham Bell and Thomas Watson were experimenting at 109 Court Street on what was to be an early version of the telephone. Bell, in a room upstairs, began to sing into the transmitter while Watson, out of earshot, listened to the receiver. Bell wrote:

> Transmitted *vocal sounds* for the very first time . . . with some modification I hope we may be able to distinguish . . . the 'timbre' of the sound. Should this be so, conversation via voice by telegraph will be a fait accompli (*Alexander Bell and the Conquest of Solitude*, 1973).

The sounds of a human voice had been transmitted over wires for the first time in Scollay Square. Because of this monumental achievement, the shop at 109 Court Street was later dismantled under the guidance of Thomas Watson and reconstructed at the telephone company's office in Post Office Square. Today, a plaque placed in front of the John F. Kennedy federal building in Government Center commemorates the site of Bell and Watson's success.

The Steaming Tea Kettle

The huge brass tea kettle, hung by the Oriental Tea Company in 1875, is a perfect example of a piece of Boston's "other" history. This landmark, along with those of more solid historical reputation, such as the Paul Revere House or the Old North Church, has been a popular tourist stop for many years. Scollay Square, which in coming years would flip its lid over the likes of Ann Corio and Sally Keith, took a great interest in the amount of liquid held under the lid of the mammoth tea kettle. An 1875 *Boston Post* article provides details of the tea kettle's story:

The question as to the capacity of the huge copper tea-kettle used by the Oriental Tea Company as a sign at their establishment on Court Street was settled at noon yesterday. Probably no local event in the past six months has excited more general curiosity than this. Certainly at least twelve thousand people found it sufficient to induce them to register a guess, and judging by the rush to the office of the company during yesterday fore noon, had the competition remained open for a week longer the list estimate would have been more than doubled.

Long before the hour set for the test to commence people began to congregate in front of the store, and by twelve o'clock the street was so thronged that it was with any difficulty that horse carts and teams made their way along.

A platform had been erected around the kettle and as Mr. Reed, the city sealer of Weights and Measures, accompanied by Messrs. Hicks and Badger, the makers of the huge affair, and the umpire Judge Baldwin, took their places upon it the excitement became great.

A temporary covering had been placed around the stage, hiding the kettle from view for a few minutes, which caused a ripple of murmurs below; but when the shield was removed, the cover of the kettle taken off and the head and shoulders of a 12 year old boy appeared above the rim, the expressions of dissatisfactions were turned into audible smiles and the multitude were in quite good humor for what was to follow.

A second youth came from the kettle and there was a shout; a third boy, and a yell; a fourth urchin and the applause was deafening. A slight interval followed and a fifth biped as large as the others emerged through the mouth. A sixth followed, and the legion below grew wild. When the seventh boy appeared many turned pale; the crowd had evidently lost its power of expression.

But there was still another to come — the eighth; and when they all stood in a row and bowed to the throng below, cheer after cheer was given them.

All thought the measuring was now to commence, but Mr. Reed again raised the lid and another head appeared above the level of the top, this one crowned with a smoothly polished beaver hat. Gradually the form arose; and the enthusiasm of the lookers-on proportionally increased when a man more than six feet tall stepped from the kettle and stood with the boys who had preceded him from the cavernous receptacle.

Mr. Reed now began his work of measuring at seven minutes past twelve o'clock, and continued with a five gallon measure up to the two hundred and twenty fifth gallon, the wonder of the crowd growing as the figures increased.

At 225 on the blackboard the largest measure was discarded, and the throng knew that the result was at hand.

It was then 1 o'clock, and as the single gallon measure was resorted to, each turn of the measure was watched by eager eyes, no word of mouth reaching the ears of those about the ponderous vessel. Two of these and they came to quarts.

"Keep perfectly still," was the caution of Mr. Shapleigh to his companions on the stage.

One quart, two quarts, then a pint, a single pint, a gill, and a stir below. A second gill was marked on the board. A third gill and the kettle was full to the brim. The measures were set aside. The result — 227 gallons, 2 quarts, 1 pint, 3 gills — was displayed on the board, and prolonged applause went up from the street as the thousands of disappointed ones scattered in every direction.

The nearest estimate to the capacity of the kettle was 227 gallons, 2 quarts, and 1 pint, or within 3 gills of the exact quantity. The above estimate was made by eight parties (*Boston Post*, January 2, 1875).

The kettle was moved several times as the buildings it was attached to were torn down to make way for Government Center. It eventually made its way back to Scollay Square, where it hangs today, still steaming, over the entrance to The Steaming Kettle coffee shop.

The Winthrop Statue and Public Transportation

September 17, 1880, was a proud day in Boston, 250th anniversary of the city's founding. To commemorate the event, the city dedicated a statue honoring the leader of the settlers and first governor of Massachusetts, John Winthrop.

The statue was a bronze replica of the marble original that stood in Statuary Hall in the Capitol building in Washington, D.C. Originally sculpted by noted artist Richard Saltonstall Greenough, the statue was placed in the middle of Scollay Square, where it was surrounded by a crisscrossing maze of trolley tracks. This location was only the first for the statue, however, as it soon became the victim of Scollay Square's increasing traffic woes.

When trolleys were horse-drawn, the biggest transportation problem the city faced was dealing with what the horses left behind. Though they did not suffer mechanical breakdowns, horse-drawn trolleys had other drawbacks. Writing about a trolley ride he took in Boston on July 18, 1883, Thomas Edison provides an interesting look at public transportation back then:

Took Street Gondola, arrived near top of Hanover Street when horses were unable to pull cars to the top of the hill, car slipped back. The executive department of my body was about to issue an order of ejectment when some of the passengers jumped out and stopped car (*Diary of Thomas Edison*, 1968).

The introduction of electric trolley cars in 1889 may have solved the street cleaning problem, but it did little to ease the growing traffic. Only six years later, the city was faced with such a horrendous traffic problem that some days it would take trolleys on Tremont Street almost an hour to move one block. After much discussion and political wrangling, the Massachusetts legislature finally agreed in 1895 to begin construction of America's first subway. In 1897 the line was extended into Scollay Square. Above ground the trolleys continued to run while workmen labored below the street.

The finished subway station at Scollay Square was truly a work of art. Called kiosks by some, pillboxes by others, stations like Scollay Square's were magnificent examples of the attention to detail that used to be paid to public structures. Even the clock worked. The Scollay Square station would someday gain fame as part of a song about a man named Charlie who went for a ride on the Boston subway one day but couldn't get off because he didn't have the exit fare of five cents. Originally a campaign song for an anti-exit fare candidate for city office, "The MTA Song" became a national hit in 1956 when the Kingston Trio sang:

> Charlie's wife goes down to the Scollay Square Station
> Every day at a quarter past two,
> And through the open window she hands Charlie a sandwich
> As the train goes rumblin' through!
> ("The MTA Song," © 1956 Atlantic Music Corp. © renewed 1984)

So what does all this have to do with the Winthrop statue? Simply this: Engineers determined that the best place for the subway entrance would be in the middle of the Square, directly over the spot where the statue originally stood. This required moving the governor thirty feet down Court Street, facing the old State House. This arrangement lasted until 1904, when the East Boston Subway tunnel was constructed. Court Street station was the designated end-of-the-line for trains making the run under the harbor. Another exit kiosk had to be built for all the extra passengers that were anticipated. The city determined that the best place for the new kiosk would be where the Winthrop statue had just been moved.

The Boston Board of Aldermen finally got the message. The streets of Scollay Square were no place for a defenseless statue, so they made plans to move it to more stable surroundings. Their first choice was City Square in Charlestown. Winthrop, they reasoned, had lived there before moving across the harbor in search of a fresh-water spring. But the Boston Board of Arts Commissioners overrode that selection and accepted an offer of a parcel of land from the First Church on Marlborough Street. John Winthrop was one of the founding members of the church in 1630, making this an equally appropriate choice. This decision would also keep the statue in Boston.

At a cost of five hundred dollars, John Winthrop, like so many of his Brahmin descendants, moved to the Back Bay. The statue was placed in a specially designed setting where it graced the church grounds for many uneventful years. The saga continues, however. In 1968, during a fire that destroyed the church, a wall collapsed and fell onto the statue, knocking the governor off his pedestal. When the statue hit the ground the force of the impact separated the governor's head from the rest of his body. And if this indignity wasn't enough, someone was caught trying to make off with the head.

During the church's reconstruction, the body was stored in Quincy while the head remained in a church office. The plan to place the statue in front of the rebuilt church was put on hold while a brief battle took place between the church and some citizens who felt the statue belonged in Winthrop Square, located in another part of the city. After the parishioners won this skirmish, the statue was repaired and placed in front of the main entrance of the church, where it stands today.

As it turns out, the Winthrop statue outlasted the subway kiosk that replaced it. Increased automobile traffic caused the city to widen Court Street in the 1920s.

Scollay Square in 1883, a vibrant commercial and transportation center. The statue of Governor Winthrop, in the lower right-hand corner of the photograph, stoically endures the clatter of horse-drawn trolleys making their way through the Square (Courtesy of the Bostonian Society/Old State House).

The Winthrop statue, dedicated on September 17, 1880 to commemorate the founding of Boston, is a replica of the marble original which still stands in the Capitol Building in Washington, D.C. (Courtesy of the Bostonian Society/Old State House).

Electric trolleys, installed in 1887, make their way through Scollay Square while workmen below construct the newest portion of America's first subway in 1897. On the right, just beyond the Crawford House, is the Oriental Tea Company where, hanging over the front door, is the original Steaming Tea Kettle (Courtesy of Robert Stanley).

The Scollay Square subway station as it appeared during the mid-1920s, some years after Scollay Square had been added as a new stop along America's first subway system. Called a kiosk by some, a pillbox by others, it was an imposing and grandiose addition to the Square (Courtesy of Robert Stanley).

Underground at the newly completed Scollay Square Station in 1898. This place was made famous by the Kingston Trio in 1964 when they sang, "Charlie's wife goes down to the Scollay Square Station every day at a quarter past two, and through the open window she hands Charlie a sandwich as the train goes rumblin' through" ("The M.T.A. Song," 1956) (Photo courtesy of the M.B.T.A.).

The Winthrop statue's first move (several dozen yards down Court Street) was forced by the construction in 1898 of the large kiosk in Scollay Square. The statue was forced to retreat completely from the Square when the smaller exit kiosk (just to the left of the large kiosk) was constructed in 1904 (Trustees of the Boston Public Library).

Thirty years after the Winthrop statue was moved to make way for the kiosk, the subway entrance itself was replaced by this simple hole in the ground. This entrance was also known as the "Canada Point" by paperboys whose supply of newspapers were dropped off here by delivery trucks. (This Depression-era photograph also shows the Hemenway Building, which at this time housed, among other things, Ligget's Drug Store. This was the site, in 1789, of the Ingersoll Home where George Washington stayed during his visit to Boston.) (Courtesy of the Bostonian Society/Old State House).

Widening Court Street helped to increase traffic flow through the Square but did nothing to alleviate the hazard created by the imposing kiosk: drivers could not see around it, putting pedestrians crossing the street in danger of being hit.

In 1927, less than thirty years after it was erected, the city tore down the stylish kiosk and replaced it with a simple hole in the ground. For many commuters, faced with more and more of these look-alike subway stations, the loss was hard to take. Perhaps no city before or since had a more elegant way of getting its citizens to work.

The Boston Police Strike of 1919

Pemberton Square housed the Suffolk County Courthouse and Boston Police Department headquarters. For many years, that meant that Scollay Square enjoyed a greater presence of policemen than the average neighborhood. The proximity of the courthouse, city hall, and the statehouse virtually assured visitors to this part of town that there would almost always be a cop around when you needed one. That was true until September 9, 1919, the day that the Boston Police Department went on strike, leaving the city without police protection for the first time since its creation.

When the Boston Police Department aligned itself with the American Federation of Labor, Police Chief Edwin Curtis made his feelings known by declaring that "no man can serve two masters," and suspended nineteen members of the force who had joined the union. The rest of the department threatened to walk off the job if they were not reinstated, something Curtis refused to consider. On the night of September 9, 1919, only thirty out of a possible four hundred officers scheduled for work showed up for duty, leaving the city virtually unprotected. For the next two days Boston was in the hands of unruly mobs who rioted and looted many parts of the city. One of the areas worst hit was Scollay Square.

The evening began normally enough, when some of the officers who remained at their posts at Station Two on Court Street were sent to Howard Street to check on a possible assault. What they found instead was a large crowd watching a crap game. After warning the players against gambling, the policemen wisely decided not to try and arrest anyone and began to walk back to Station Two. On any other night, the incident would have ended here. Tonight, however, the crowd followed them, yelling taunts and shouting "Scabs!" as they walked through the Square. The officers made it inside the station, which was promptly surrounded by hundreds of people who had joined the taunting mob. An attempt by the precinct captain and some of his men to disperse the crowd failed, and they retreated back into the station. The crowd was growing, drawing passers-by like a magnet, and soon there were almost a thousand people milling around the Square.

Then someone threw a rock through the window of a cigar store on Tremont Row. Within minutes the crowd emptied the store of all its merchandise. Then they moved down Scollay Square to Hanover Street, where they rushed the doors of the Casino Theatre. Several made it inside, where they tore posters from the walls and yelled at the actors, many of whom seemed truly afraid of what might happen next.

But the rioters soon left the Casino and began a crap game in the middle of Hanover Street. A policeman who had been following them tried to stop the game but ended up in a fight with some of the participants. Somehow the officer managed to get away, which left the street under the complete control of the crowd.

Then the front window of the Lewis Shoe Store was broken and soon every shoe was in the hands (or on the feet) of the mob. They moved unchecked down Hanover to Washington Street, assaulting or robbing anyone unlucky enough to get in their way, until they found themselves in front of the Wholesale Provision Company. A member of the crowd tossed a brick through the front window, bringing out the night watchman, who had been in the basement of the store. This was no ordinary night watchman, however.

James J. Burns had spent half of his seventy years on the police force and was not about to let an unruly mob have its way with his employer's stock. "Get back there," he yelled while waving his .38 revolver, "or I'll send you before your God!" (*Boston Post*, September 10, 1919). For about twenty minutes a tense standoff took place between the crowd and Burns. Slowly the crowd dispersed, and the last of them finally moved back to Hanover Street. There they looted the less-protected Puritan Clothing Store.

Continuing to Sudbury Street they made quick work of the Coleman and Keating bottling company. By now it was almost midnight, and the crowd, believing it had complete control of this part of the city, returned to Court Street:

> Failure of the police authorities to provide adequate protection for Boston in the opening hours of the strike was atoned for in a measure by the personal bravery of Supt. of Police Michael Crowley, who alone and unafraid held a mob of 1000 rioters at bay at Court Street and Pemberton Square as the gangsters surged and threatened his life if he did not release a prisoner caught in the act of looting.
>
> Undaunted, his hat missing, Supt. Crowley stood firm with drawn pistol and shouted:
>
> "I'll blow out the brains of the first man to move. Come on you __damn cowards."
>
> The deadliness of the official's intent held the crowd in check. In another moment a crowd of six inspectors swung around the corner and escorted the prisoner to headquarters.
>
> Then Crowley drew the crowd back, step by step, with threats of shooting to kill (*Boston Record American*, September 10, 1919).

Until this point in the evening, the crowd had met little official resistance. But this show of strength was enough to convince them to abandon Scollay Square. They moved downtown to Washington Street where they continued their rampage until about one-thirty that morning.

Assessed damage from the night was about $200,000. Mayor Peters, furious with the evening's activity, took control of the police department, determined not to let hoodlums have their way with his city for a second day. With help from Governor Calvin Coolidge he arranged for a police force consisting of the State Cavalry, the Massachusetts State Guard, Harvard University students, and Metropolitan Police. Though strong in number, this makeshift police force did not have a good day in Scollay Square.

The Square's proximity to police headquarters, the governor's office, city hall, and Station Two made it a natural gathering place for people to view the events surrounding America's first police strike. By two o'clock in the afternoon almost five thousand people had filled the streets of Scollay Square.

Suddenly a fight broke out at the Walton Lunch Company at 9 Tremont Row. Before anyone could stop the fracas, the front window of the luncheonette was broken, bringing the manager to the front door with a revolver, which he waved at the crowd. When police arrived to arrest the window breaker they were pelted with large lumps of coal taken from a passing wagon. Two of the officers were knocked down, and a few men in the crowd began to yell "Let's get 'em, let's get the cops!" (*Boston Post*, September 11, 1919). Luckily, before any harm could come to the injured policemen, two more armed officers arrived and drove the crowd back into the street.

More and more people continued to fill the area, and by late afternoon there were almost ten thousand people in Scollay Square. Though many were content to watch, others were busy breaking windows, looting stores, and assaulting passers-by. As the afternoon wore on, the police found themselves unable to control the throngs. It was now about six-thirty in the evening, and over on Cornhill several members of the volunteer police force, among them "Tacks" Hardwick, a popular Harvard halfback recruited by the mayor, were dangerously close to losing their lives against a mob of night stick-wielding thugs.

Just as Superintendent Crowley was about to lead a rescue attempt down Cornhill, the sound of hoof beats could be heard from the direction of Pemberton Square. The First Troop of the cavalry, led by Captain Frederick Hunneman, was moving swiftly down the hill and positioning itself by the subway kiosk, facing Scollay Square. Francis Russel, in his book on the police strike, described the scene:

> There was a moment of silence, then a sharp command, and with pennons flying and sabres flashing in the wan afternoon light, the clink of chain bits and the clatter of hooves, the troopers charged. The crowd wavered and broke, then panicked. Oddly enough, there were even a few cheers as the cavalry trotted by. Dividing, the troop formed platoon fronts, one platoon forcing a segment of the crowd toward Howard Street, the other driving the rest down Court Street, Cornhill and Brattle Street (*A City in Terror 1919: The Boston Police Strike*, 1975).

Within minutes, Scollay Square was cleared. The guardsmen, now in command of the Square, patrolled in smaller groups. But the crowd had still not gone home. Instead, they congregated on the edge of the Square in smaller groups of several hundred a piece. One gang broke into the Market Men's Shop on Washington Street. By the time police arrived, the looters and most of the store's merchandise were gone.

The cavalry had to move on to other sections of the city, which left the Square

Scollay Square on the afternoon of September 10, 1919, during the Boston Police Strike. Soon after this picture was taken, a regiment of cavalry stormed the Square (Trustees of the Boston Public Library).

open to the public again. It wasn't long before most of the ten thousand returned to the Square where they milled around, apparently satisfied to be back in the center of the excitement. Then, around seven-thirty, as policemen pursued a crowd of gamblers up Howard Street, shots rang out and a man fell dead. The police claimed he was shot in the chest by someone in the crowd who, while running away, turned and fired, mistaking the man for an officer. But the word quickly spread throughout Scollay Square that the police had shot a man in the back. This was all the encouragement the mob needed.

First the windows of Woolworth's department store were broken, followed by the breaking of several smaller storefronts on Tremont Row and Court Street. Young boys who had climbed on top of the subway kiosk were using their position to launch more missiles into store windows. Clumps of mud "landed in the faces of volunteer policemen, the mob each time bellowing its appreciation of the adaptation from the squash pie comedy of the movies" (*Boston Post*, September 11, 1919). The mob was so large that the police could not get anywhere near the window breakers. Often the crowd would part to give a stone thrower a clear shot at his target, only to close up around him when a policeman tried to make an arrest.

Automobiles and trucks that had blundered into the Square were either pelted with rocks and coal or simply forced to stop. A mail truck was almost turned over, but somehow the police were able to prevent that from happening.

Men in the windows of the Crawford House and places of business repeatedly remarked, as the evening wore on, that the mob scene staged in the muddy square in the shadow of the State House was absolutely beyond their imaginations. The disrespect for the mounted troopers, who were cut and injured, the inhumanity of the hoodlums and the wholesale disregard for life appeared like a scene from some ferocious pageant (*Boston Post*, September 11, 1919).

Between nine and ten o'clock that night an ambulance made four trips into Scollay Square to remove wounded soldiers, cavalry, and citizens. The sight of the ambulance did little to slow the crowd's frenzy, however, and windows continued to be broken and stores looted until around ten o'clock. That's when the state guard made its final assault on the Square.

Two companies with fixed bayonets formed into squares. Led by the cavalry they forced their way into the Square and drove the crowd down the side streets until the area was devoid of people. Most of the dispersed crowd went home, while others went downtown where they continued their rampage for several hours.

The next morning Scollay Square woke to find armed militiamen stationed every ten feet along Court Street. To prevent crowds from forming, pedestrians were not allowed to stand still in any one spot for longer than a minute. And although incidents between the militia and citizens were few and far between, one soldier did leave a legacy in Scollay Square. It seems that the guardsman accidentally fired his weapon, hitting a PAINLESS DENTIST sign. This incident became known among the militia as the "Battle of the Signs." It may have been the only shot fired in Scollay Square after the militia took over.

In any case, the danger of further looting and rioting was over. Within several weeks a new force was recruited and control of the city returned to the police. Store windows were repaired, merchandise replaced, and eventually the Square returned to normal. But there are still people alive today who cannot forget that fantastic night when the cavalry charged Scollay Square.

The Last Transformation

For Scollay Square, returning to normal would be difficult given the fact that Prohibition, which had been ratified early in 1919, would soon become law. With the coming of the 1920s a lot of Scollay Square's activity moved underground into speakeasies. There weren't necessarily more of these ginjoints here than in any other part of the city; it just seemed that way given the Square's reputation. The sailors and the students and the curious still found their way into the many lunch-eonettes, grilles, drugstores, tattoo parlors, pawnshops, and theaters. They just had to look a little harder (but not much harder) to find something stronger to drink than a Moxie.

The next two decades, much like the mid- and late 1800s, were a time of great change in the general character of Scollay Square. Whereas in the 1850s and 1860s the Square made the transition from erudite to commonplace, and in the 1880s and 1890s moved full speed from commonplace to bawdy, it was during the 1920s and 1930s that it slid inexorably from bawdy to tawdry. Part of this can be attributed to the economic upheavals created by Prohibition and the Great Depression. But it was also due to the new political and social climate in Boston made possible by the rise of the Irish. Certainly none of them had a greater impact than James Michael Curley.

Elected to the office of mayor three times between 1914 and 1930, Curley saw his rise to power as a way for the Irish, who had suffered greatly under Yankee domination for two generations, to reap the social, recreational, and medical benefits he felt they (and other minorities) had been denied in Boston. Thomas H. O'Connor wrote this about Curley's motives and the impact he had on the Square:

> Curley left the inner city . . . to wallow in its Puritan self-righteousness, and turned his attention and his municipal favors during the 1920s and 1930s to the "other" Boston which never failed to give him their devotion — and their votes. While he built playgrounds in Dorchester and Roxbury, Scollay Square turned into a place where ugly tattoo parlors and sleazy burlesque houses blighted the historic land-scape. . . . The idea of improving "new" Boston with money extracted from "old" Boston obviously struck Curley as a particularly appropriate way of balancing the scales which had, for so long, been weighted against the people he represented (*Bibles, Brahmins, and Bosses: A Short History of Boston*, 1984).

And so it was that Scollay Square began the slide that, except for a brief economic jolt during the Second World War, led to the disrepair and blight of the 1950s. Though people would continue to patronize the Square during the 1920s and 1930s, its heyday had obviously passed.

What probably kept the Square from dying completely during the dry days of Prohibition and the terrible years of the Depression was a theater. Not just any theater, but the Old Howard, a burlesque house whose history deserves a telling all its own.

The Old Howard Theatre, around the turn of the century (Courtesy of the Bostonian Society/Old State House).

The Old Howard

I t started in a blaze of religious fervor and ended more than a century later when a real fire gutted its grand frame. The demolition of its granite walls saw the end of America's oldest theater: the Howard Athenaeum, later known as the Old Howard. On its stage the great dramatists of the nineteenth century, such as Edmund Kean and Junius Booth, performed classic plays of the English language. Later, Weber and Fields, Fred Allen, and Fanny Brice would create their own classics in vaudeville. The stage would be visited last by burlesque stars who entertained generations of servicemen, Harvard undergrads, high school truants, and bald-headed men.

The Howard and the End of the World

One of Boston's greatest ironies is that its most infamous theater began as a church built expressly for the end of the world. Adventist minister William Miller had spent a lifetime studying the scriptures. He had paid particular attention to the Book of Revelation and, with his flair for mathematics, calculated that April 23, 1843, was to be Judgment Day. One hundred years later the event was described for readers of the *American Mercury*:

> This was to be no abstract matter, but a literal end to the world, the day of Jubilee, when all on earth except the sanctified were to be destroyed in a Holocaust of fire. Gabriel was to wind his horn. The graves would yawn. And Christ almighty would walk among the saved ones (*American Mercury*, April 1944).

Miller was not the fire and brimstone sort, preferring to state his "facts" calmly and let the people decide. Working alongside him, though, was Elder Knapp, who more than made up for Miller's lack of zeal. While the two preached at separate churches on Chardon Street, sympathetic pastors from Boston and New York began circulating a horribly descriptive paper called "The Midnight Cry." Soon there were thousands of loyal converts (called Millerites by the skeptical press) listening to these voices of doom.

A huge tabernacle was built on Howard Street by the Millerites in the early 1840s. (Howard Street was originally Southack's Court, after British naval captain Cyprian Southack, who owned a home there in the early eighteenth century. It was renamed in the early nineteenth century for philanthropist John Howard.) Within the wooden church the Millerites gathered to await the end of the world. Inside were murals depicting grotesque monsters as described in the Revelation. The devotees, who had sold their possessions and closed up their businesses, crowded inside the church and prayed with an almost insane fervor, some shrieking in agony waiting for April 23 to arrive.

Not everyone felt the tug of Armageddon. On the appointed day many Bostonians calmly picnicked on the Common, watching for the ascension of the white-robed Millerites, whom they figured would first have to crash through the tabernacle's roof. That didn't happen, of course, for as mathematically gifted as Miller might have been, he was certainly wrong this time. He recalculated and came up with a new date—October 18, 1847. But by March of 1844, most of the Millerites had deserted the tabernacle and were attempting to get back some of what they had given away in their religious fever. Miller himself returned home to Vermont later that year and the movement died away.

The Church Becomes a Theater

Several Millerites managed to recoup some of their losses by leasing the tabernacle to a theatrical company. The front of the building was covered with a granite facade, while inside a full-sized stage replaced the altar. There was no balcony or box seating, and every ticket cost fifty cents. On October 13, 1845, Sheridan's *School for Scandal* opened at the newly named Howard Athenaeum. Why Athenaeum? Walter Muir Whitehill explains:

A lingering Puritan prejudice against the supposed wickedness of the stage had caused Boston theatre operators to choose names that implied intellectual elevation. The promoters of the theatre on Howard Street made use of a classical name familiar since 1807 because of the Boston Athenaeum, although they supplied no books for protective coloration (*The Metamorphosis of Scollay and Bowdoin Squares*, 1973).

Running afoul of the law by putting on a play was something that had happened many times in Boston, long before the Howard was even a church. Coincidentally, it was *School for Scandal* that was performed at Boston's first theater in 1792 when the sheriff arrested all the actors for "a serious crime" (*American Mercury*, April 1944). Only two years later, however, the Boston Theatre on Federal Street opened without interruption from the law. By the time the Howard Athenaeum opened, there were several theaters doing business in Boston. All of Boston's major papers at the time ran ads for them, and two even carried reviews, such as this one:

> The Howard Athenaeum, a new candidate for patronage of the public, will be open tonight with a capital bill. The old Tabernacle has been transformed into a very convenient and handsome theatre and it would sadly puzzle a Millerite to imagine himself at home in its now tasteful interior. Of the company, we can better speak after having seen one of their performances but the names of several old favorites warrant us in expecting good things. That the house will be crowded tonight to the utmost strength of its capacity may be considered certain (*Boston Courier*, October 13, 1845).

The reviews were favorable, and during the next few months the house was usually full. On February 23, 1846, the audience was enjoying the play *Piazarro*, which climaxes with a ball of flames descending from the rafters. This time the ball dropped onto the stage, and started a fire. No one was hurt, but the fire spread through the wooden structure and completely destroyed it, save for the granite facade.

The lot remained empty (except for its use by a traveling circus that spring) while plans were made for a new theater to be built with Quincy granite. The architect was Isaiah Rogers, who had designed the Astor House in New York and the Maxwell House in Nashville. On July 4, 1846, the cornerstone was laid for the three-story structure.

Mr. Boyd and Mr. Beard, two entreprenuers who funded the construction, obviously had only so much faith in dramatic entertainment, for they also had a brewery built on the first floor to help supplement the theater's revenue.

> The Otis S. Neal brewery continued to bottle ale and beer at a lively pace day and night. Heavy brewery wagons drawn by draft horses rumbled down Howard Street behind the society broughams of first-nighters. To keep the yeasty fumes of the bottling works from the patrons, the management installed special ventilators (*Colliers*, September 30, 1950).

That's why patrons of the Howard Athenaeum, after paying their admission, always had to walk up a flight of stairs to reach the orchestra level. Once there,

> Patrons found a "truly elegant playhouse." The orchestra was surrounded by sharply rising tiers of seats. Three tiers of boxes rose one above the other, all fancy with cast

iron grillwork, and whitewashed. Three horseshoe balconies rose to the ceiling, from the center of which hung a gigantic gaslight (*American Mercury*, April, 1944).

Among the other amenities were cushioned seats, a first for Boston theater. Settling into these seats on the evening of October 5, 1846, Boston saw its first show at the new Howard Athenaeum, *The Rivals*, a drawing room comedy. The new structure had one big advantage over its wooden predecessor: the balconies and orchestra seats allowed the manager, James Hackett, to charge different prices depending upon where one sat.

If there was any disadvantage to popularity, it could be seen in newspaper reports and commentaries that appeared soon after the theater opened:

The managers of the Howard Athenaeum would greatly improve the alterations of that elegant place of amusement if they should adopt measures to keep the steps and sidewalk in front of the house clear of loafers that so frequently obstruct ingress and egress into the theatre (*Boston Daily Courier*, October 9, 1846).

At the Howard, Mlle. Blangy, a dancer of much repute commences tonight with a ballet of La Giselle. We have received a note in which it is said "As it is thought there will be great anxiety to witness Mlle. Blangy's performance of Giselle this evening at the Howard Athenaeum persons are cautioned against purchasing tickets which may be offered for sale about the doors of the theatre. Several persons who passed the doorkeeper on the opening night without delivering their tickets have offered

A rare look inside the Old Howard, as seen in the late forties or early fifties (From the collection of Leo Ajemian).

them for sale. They will not admit holders to the house" (*Boston Daily Mail*, October 12, 1846).

Imagine that. The Howard wasn't even open a week, and already there were ticket scalpers. Boston's highbrow obviously did not consider the scalpers or the higher prices to be a deterrent because they made the Howard even more popular than it had been before the fire. Here Boston heard its first Italian grand opera and saw the first American performance of the ballet *Giselle*. James Hackett even imported a troupe of Viennese dancers, who delighted audiences at the Howard. The list of actors who trod its boards reads like a who's who of nineteenth-century theater. Junius Booth played Hamlet, and each of his four sons (including John Wilkes) performed before the Howard's kerosene footlights. William MacReady, the great Shakespearean actor, also played Hamlet. Appearances by Mr. and Mrs. Charles Kean, Cora Mowatt, Edwin Forrest, Charlotte Cushman, E. L. Davenport, and others allowed the Howard to proudly boast in its advertisements:

> As Rome points proudly to her Coliseum,
> So Boston treats her Howard Athenaeum.

But by the time of the Civil War, Boston was no longer treating the Athenaeum with the respect and patronage to which it was accustomed. Management lowered the price for general admission in an attempt to shore up a sagging box office. The drawing room comedies and one act plays, which, in the 1840s and 1850s, helped make the Howard one of Boston's most popular playhouses, no longer satisfied the theater-going public.

The simple fact was, that by the late 1800s, the Howard was no longer located in an exclusively aristocratic section of Boston. Though Beacon Hill (with its ever-present Brahmin population) hadn't changed, the North and West Ends were now inhabited by a new breed of Bostonian: mostly immigrant, working-class Irish. The more the streets surrounding the Howard changed, the less inclined Boston's upper crust was to venture down the Hill, and the new Bostonians apparently cared little for the Howard's bill of fare. The managers realized that something had to be done to save their business.

The Howard Goes Public

The beginning of a new era for the Howard, that of popular entertainment, was signaled by advertisements appearing in Boston papers on August 10, 1868. These ads touted acrobats, jugglers, and dancers. Even though private boxes were still available, it was now possible to get into the gallery for only fifteen cents. Instead of *Giselle* and Mozart, there were minstrel shows and pantomime. Instead of the

Booth family, there was Buffalo Bill Cody and his "mammoth combination of 25 first class artists" riding their horses onstage (*Colliers*, September 30, 1950).

Manager John B. Stetson brought in acts that soon made the Howard Boston's number-one popular theater. There was the first Human Fly, who walked on the ceiling of the Howard and made jokes about the bald-headed men who occupied the orchestra seats. (Yes, even back then it seems you had be a bald-headed man to get a front row seat at the Howard.) Tony Pastor, a noted comedian with his own company, also performed. John L. Sullivan, on his way to the world boxing championship, took on all comers in a makeshift ring on the Howard stage, almost killing Professor Mike Donovan one night. *A Dark Secret*, a play presented in early 1883, promised a "thrilling tale of the Thames Valley, with marvelous aquatic scenes—the Henly Regatta, presented with Real Sailboats, Rowboats, Racing Shells and Steam Launches, the Stage Being Flooded with 5,000 Cubic Feet of Water" (*American Mercury*, April 1944).

Even the programs were given new life. Printed on purple paper, they carried an advertisement asking people to "Come where the woodbine twineth at 19 Howard Street." This was the address of a saloon that advertised, "The Brass Gong in our Refectory sounds two minutes before the Curtain goes up on the next act," in case any theater lovers lost track of time between drinks.

The brewery continued operation in the Howard's basement. Several times the fumes got so bad that the theater's ventilation system had be overhauled. These repairs solved the odor problem but did little to cool the theater during the hot summer. Thomas Alva Edison, who had left Scollay Square a few years earlier, was vacationing in nearby Swampscott when he made the following entry in his diary, dated July 18, 1883:

> Went to the theatre, where we found it very hot. Solomon the composer came from the cellar of fairies and sprung a chestnut overture on the few mortals in the audience chamber.
>
> Then the curtain arose showing the usual number of servant girls in tights. The raising of the panapoly of fairyland let some more heat in—a rushing was heard and Dora said they were turning on the steam. The fairies mopped their foreheads, perspiration dripped down the stage from the painted cherubs over the arch.
>
> After numerous military evocations by the chorus Miss Lillian Russel made her appearance. Beautiful costume, sweet voice. Wore a fur lined coat which I thought about as appropriate in this weather as to clothe the foreman on the Red Sea Steamers in seacokin' overcoats.
>
> Our seats were in the baldheaded section (*The Diary of Thomas Alva Edison*, 1968).

In the early 1890s, a man named G. E. Lothrop became manager. His first official act was to suspend the custom of seat checks, which were used by thirsty patrons who wished to leave the theater and saunter over to a local pub and have one or two drinks between acts. Despite the combined efforts of area tavern owners to persuade him to reverse his decision, Mr. Lothrop refused to continue the tradition. That night, when the curtain went up, a ten-piece brass band suddenly stood up near the front row and began to play loudly. Lothrop got the message, and the next night seat checks were given out. No attempt was ever made again to stop the practice.

Lothrop's other managerial decisions fared better. During his tenure, the Howard booked such stars as Weber and Fields, Maggie Cline, Gus Williams, Pat Rooney, and Harrigan and Hart. John L. Sullivan, who had become boxing's champion, now appeared in dramatic roles in melodramas like *Honest Hearts and Willing Hands.*

Though there was no longer an effort to draw the former clientele, it seemed that some members of Boston's upper crust had little problem finding their way to Howard Street. Justice Oliver Wendell Holmes, a frequent visitor to the Old Howard, remarked after one vaudevillian delivered a particularly spicy punch line, "Thank God I am a man of low taste!" (*Saturday Evening Post*, September 26, 1959).

By this time, the word *Athenaeum* had been cast aside, perhaps signaling the final step from upper crust to common man. The theater, in continuous use for almost half a century, was now known simply as the Old Howard.

The Old Howard

Following John L. Sullivan's footsteps as a take-on-all-comers boxer were Gentleman Jim Corbett, Jack Johnson, and Jack Dempsey. Dempsey, by the way, was the highest paid performer ever to appear at the Howard, receiving $5,000 for one week. Looking at the list of entertainers who worked here, one can see why Fred Allen called Howard Street "the small time actor's Broadway" (*Much Ado About Me*, 1957). Jack Pearl, Bert Lahr, Fanny Brice, Bobby Clark, Joe Penner, Phil Silvers, Abbott and Costello, and Sophie Tucker were among those who honed their skills at the Howard before making it big in movies and radio.

Long before he achieved stardom on radio, Fred Allen played the Howard as Freddie St. James, clown juggler. He recalled some of the other actors and actresses in his autobiography:

> There was Dancing Bandy, who featured his famous Bandy walks: during his final number Bandy walked in step like a fat man, a minister, a Jewish pushcart salesman, an effeminate man, a Civil War veteran and so on.
> There was Hindu Sam, the fire-eater, and his famous Hindu Basket Trick. Hindu Sam placed his small son in a small wicker basket and, after closing the top and chanting a few incantations, proceeded to thrust long swords through the basket from every possible angle without impaling the boy. Sam claimed his Hindu powers enabled him to protect his small son from harm. Sam's Hindu powers, however, could not stop his small son from growing. When the boy became too large to fit into the basket, Hindu Sam's theatrical career came to an abrupt end.

There were the Minstrel Maids, featuring Cassie French. Cassie had an enormous bust. With her short neck and protuding bosom, Cassie always looked as though she were looking over somebody else's behind. When the Minstrel Maids played the Old Howard, if there were only four men in the horseshoe balcony, they would all be huddled together at the extreme ends of the horseshoe to enjoy a birdseye view of Cassie.

Also on regular view was Tom Heffernan, a dancer who had but one leg. To keep up appearances and for the purposes of dancing, Tom wore an old style wooden leg (*Much Ado About Me*, 1957).

Also appearing at the Old Howard were the Nightingales, a singing and dancing act made up of four youngsters from New York. Joining bass Lou Levy were three brothers whose stage names were Groucho, Gummo, and Harpo Marx. In his autobiography, Harpo recalled:

I got my first laugh onstage, at the Old Howard Theatre in Boston, the famous burlesque house. We, the Nightingales in the white duck suits with the fake carnations, did a turn in the olio between shows. With hands on each other's shoulders and swaying in tempo, we sang "Mandy Lane." We were scarcely noticed during our number (even by the piano player, who concentrated on watching the clock for his dinner hour to start) until our last night there.

At the Old Howard the loges came all the way around the house, like a giant horseshoe, and the end boxes hung over the stage. On Saturday night, between burlesque shows, there were three drunks in the end box at stage right. They were loud and restless during the olio, and especially during our rendition of "Mandy Lane." In the middle of the song, I heard one of the drunks say to his pals, "Hey, lookit! Watch me get the second kid from the end."

The second kid from the end was me. He got me—with a jetstream of tobacco juice, smack down the front of my white duck jacket.

"Watch this!" said the drunk. "I'll get him again!" Before he could get me again I backed up two paces and marched to the lee side of Groucho, without losing a beat or diverting my eyes from the audience. The audience howled. They'd never seen anything funny in the olio before and probably never did again. But it wasn't funny to me—or to Minnie [Harpo's mother] who spent most of the night scrubbing tobacco-juice stain out of my costume (*Harpo Speaks*, 1961).

Having learned from experience of the public's fickle heart, management was always quick to include new forms of entertainment on the Old Howard's bill. They installed a movie screen around 1912. Fred Allen describes a typical day at the theater:

Between five and eight when the burlesque performers went out to dinner, the vaudeville acts and an old movie carried on. The burlesque shows of the era were clean and funny; the smut and strip tease came later. All the great burlesque stars appeared here, as did boxing champions, six-day bicycle riders, and other sports celebrities. The Old

1950 — 105th Season of the Old Howard — 1951

THE OLD HOWARD

A NATIONAL INSTITUTION

CONTINUOUS 9 A.M. to 11 P.M.   TEL. CA 7-1565

3 Gigantic Stage Shows Daily: 12 Noon, 2:45 P.M. and 8:30 P.M.

Four Shows Saturday: 12 Noon, 2:45 — 7:15 — 10:00 P.M.

MIDNIGHT SHOW EVERY FRIDAY NIGHT at 12 O'Clock

WEEK OF NOVEMBER 6, 1950

EXTRA ADDED ATTRACTION

The New, Undisputed Queen of Burlesque

ROSE LA ROSE

THE ORIGINAL T. N. T. GIRL

THE GIRL WHO HAS EVERYTHING

B E T T E

HOWARD

Our Feature Attraction

INIMITABLE FUN-MAKER

EDDIE INNIS

A Lesson in Levity

LADD & LYON

Nifty Little Tantalizer   Drawling Comic   Robust Straight

JANICE BROWN FRED FRAMPTON HARRY RYAN

Dainty and Demure   Songs You Love

NONA CARVER   **FRANK PETAN**

A complete program from the Old Howard in 1950, just three years before it was closed down by the city. Among the coming attractions was the movie *That Hagan Girl*, starring Ronald Reagan — the former actor's only "appearance" here (From the collection of Leo Ajemian).

Warning: Taking of photographs and candid camera shots prohibited.

PROGRAM

Dances Staged by Madeline Mixon

Scenery by Kaj Velden

Wardrobe by Eva Collins Company, Philadelphia

Music Under Direction of Arthur Geissler

Opening—"Hello Everybody" ......Frank Petan and Howardettes
Hungry Flirt ....Frampton, Ryan, Carver, Louden
Nifty Little Tantalizer ....Janice Brown
Archie the Fireman ....Innis, Ryan, Carver
Ballet "Romance" ....Mixon, Petan and Lovelies
Dainty and Demure ....Nona Carver
The Trixter with Bottle ....Frampton, Ryan, Petan
Our Feature Attraction—The Girl Who Has Everything
BETTE HOWARD
Beauty and Song ....Maddy Mixon and Howardettes
Arabella ....Innis, Ryan, Brown
A Lesson in Levity ....Ladd & Lyon
Introducing the T.N.T. Girl.........Frank Petan and Gay Nineties
Extra Added Attraction—The Queen of Burleque
ROSE LA ROSE
Finale—"Just a Flash" ....Terry Dee, Petan and Lovelies

ACT II

Once Again	Nona Carver
Riddles	Innis and Brown
Once More	BETTE HOWARD
The Flying Clock	Frampton, Ryan, Petan, Carver
Beauty Ballet	Frank Petan and Lovelies
The Race Track	Innis, Frampton, Ryan, Petan
Look, Look Again	ROSE LA ROSE
Finale	Petan and Howardettes

ON OUR SCREEN
"YOU'RE MY EVERYTHING",......Dan Dailey, Anne Baxter
"THE UNSUSPECTED"..........Joan Caulfield, Claude Rains
Latest Warner News

COMING ATTRACTIONS
SPECTACULAR HOLIDAY EVE MIDNIGHT SHOW
FRIDAY, NOV. 10 (ARMISTICE DAY EVE)
AT 12:00 MIDNIGHT
Extra Added Attractions — Seats Now on Sale

MONDAY, NOV. 20—GEORGIA SOTHERN,
LEXING AND WEST
MONDAY, NOV. 27—VICKIE WELLES,
BOB FERGUSON
MONDAY, DEC. 4—SCARLETT KELLY,
DICK RICHARDS, LINDA SCOTT, BERT CARR
MONDAY, DEC. 11—VALERIE PARKS,
STINKY AND SHORTY

NEXT WEEK

A STREAK OF LIGHTNING	CHEESE 'N CRACKERS COMIC
# Nora Ford	# Billy Hagan
THE GIRL WITH THE MILLION DOLLAR LEGS	RIOTOUS FUNSTER
## CEIL VON DELL	## HARRY BENTLEY
The Superb Sophisticate	Sensational Oriental Entertainers
JEANNETTE LEFFLER	**JIM WONG TROUPE**
A Heavenly Dream	Gabby Fellow
MARLENE MASON	**FLOYD HALLICY**

Songsation Plus
FRANK PETAN

60 RARIN' TO GO BURLESQUERS — 30 EYEFUL CUTIES

ON THE SCREEN

"THE EAGLE AND THE HAWK"..John Payne, Rhonda Fleming
"THE HAGAN GIRL"..........Ronald Reagan, Shirley Temple
Latest Warner News

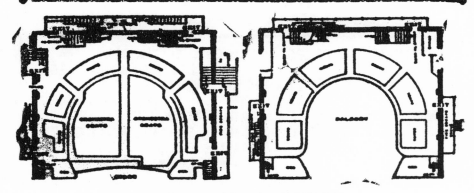

SORRY — NO SMOKING

Howard's clientele was predominantly stag, and the theatre was a popular rendezvous spot for sailors. The Charlestown Navy Yard was but an anchor's throw across the river from Howard Street, and sailors returning from long cruises invariably rushed to the Old Howard to check on the current models of female pulchritude and to see if any improvements had been made in their absence.

Gallery admission to the Old Howard was ten cents, and order was preserved in the gallery by a burly policeman carrying a billy club. Before the burlesque show started, the officer appeared in the first row of the gallery and announced loudly "Hats off! And no smoking! Keep your feet off the rails!" To convince the galleryites of his sincerity the officer smote the iron gallery rail with his billy. Metallic reverberations ensued, and for minutes no galleryite could hear a thing (*Much Ado About Me*, 1957).

By the twenties, advertisements for shows at the Old Howard heralded a new form of art, the chorus girl:

Every guy thinks that his sweetie is about the only girl in the world but you can take it from us that when your lights flash E. J. Ryan's "Round the Town Bunch" at the Old Howard you are going to forget everything else. Get ready to give them the friendly fin — they'll sure doll up and look choice. Chris Columbus discovered America and if you're a wise one you'll discover that these dolls are all lookers. They have a line of blarney that lands you in a jiffy, and it's up to you to look in and give them a gaze. Always something doing 1 to 11 at the Old Howard (*Boston Record American*, October 12, 1925).

Fred Doherty was the man responsible for this and the rest of the Howard's advertising from 1910 until his death in 1940. A short man who weighed two hundred pounds, and a real character, he was rarely seen in a suit that didn't look rumpled or without a dead stogie hanging from his mouth. "Always something doing from 1 to 11" became the Howard's famous tag line.

Striptease at the Howard

Lines of chorus girls parading across the stage of the Howard during the late 1800s evolved into individual striptease acts by the 1920s. The origin of striptease, which came to dominate the Howard stage, has never really been established, but a few possibilities are worth mentioning.

Chorus girls had for years been wearing brightly colored costumes, under which they wore tights and leotards. Sometime in the late twenties a daring few appeared onstage without the protective undercovering. One story has it that during her tap dance routine a young Chicago dancer lost the strap to her costume. The wild response from the all-male audience inspired the manager to keep that event in the show.

Another contender for the right to be called the first striptease artist was Hinda

Wassau. Hinda used to do a shimmy dance, much like the one Theda Bara did in her 1916 movie *The Vamp*. Her act concluded with her shimmy vibrating off her chorus costume, which was worn over another briefer costume. Legend has it that one night the two costumes stuck together, and when she shimmied off her upper costume the lower one went with it.

Howard management, always aiming to please its patrons, began booking women who practiced this art form in the 1920s. One young beauty who became the Howard's very own star was Ann Corio. She was responsible not only for bringing large throngs of men into the theater but a new clientele to burlesque as well: women. It was 1929, and manager Al Somerby couldn't help but notice that quite a few women came along with their husbands and boyfriends to see Ann's show. Together, he and Ann cooked up the idea of a midnight Ladies' Show for women without escorts. It was a sellout, forcing the Howard to make a small structural change: the installation of a ladies' room.

Ann Corio later wrote that while performing at the Howard, she made her mark on America's most prestigious university:

> My favorite audience was from the educational institution along the Charles River. Friday's midnight performance was Harvard's show of shows. How those boys would howl. They took possession of me. I was their girl, and around the circuit, wherever there were other colleges I was known as "Harvard's baby."
>
> I had fans in the faculty, too. An astronomy professor asked his class to name a heavenly body. One student yelled out "Ann Corio." An anthropology teacher, Professor Hooten, asked me to visit his home and have tea with the family.
>
> There I was having tea, if you please, with an academic great. We discussed anthropology. Did I think beauty was hereditary? Was it inherited from one's parents? I answered these and other questions for a while and then I asked *him* a question. "Professor, how can you explain the great amount of deafness in Boston?"
>
> "Deafness? I didn't know we had an excessive amount."
>
> I said there must be, because night after night hundreds of people at the Old Howard asked for front row seats. They claimed to be "hard of hearing" (*This Was Burlesque*, 1968).

So many students ventured across the Charles that some called the Old Howard the "Old Harvard." One night a group of undergrads spotted their Latin professor sitting directly in front of them enjoying the show. Soon the professor noticed his students. With little acknowledgment of the ticklish situation, he calmly turned to them and said, "Why the whole thing is straight out of Plautus and Terrence!" (*Saturday Evening Post*, September 26, 1959).

The Howard Is "Banned in Boston"

By the thirties the Howard was truly the people's playhouse and the bane of those overseers of Boston's morals, the Watch and Ward Society. A private group incorporated in 1884 under the name "New England Society for the Supression of Vice," they were the determined upholders of "public morality and the removal of corrupting agencies" (*North American Review*).

The Watch and Ward Society naturally kept a close eye on proceedings at the Old Howard. The group's support in Boston was no doubt enhanced by muckraking newspapers like the *Searchlight*. "HOWARD THE SHAME OF BOSTON," the headline screamed in 1916. The paper told of the "flimsy attire of the women" and of the "innovation of standing all the women upon the stage in a semicircle and having each one in turn make her debut to the audience by making a smutty remark" (*Harvard Magazine*, November 1973). There is no record to indicate if the paper was able to keep patrons away, although speculation is that the free advertising actually did wonders for the box office.

The Watch and Ward Society did triumph, if only briefly, when it succeeded in closing the Howard for thirty days in 1933. The Society had sent representatives into the theater for five months to observe the shows and gather evidence. They then compelled Mayor James Michael Curley to hold a hearing of the Board of Censors to determine if the Howard should lose its license. For those who appreciate stories of the Old Howard and of former mayor and Boston legend James Michael Curley, the hearing certainly ranks as one of the most amusing examples of each.

The City Board of Censors was a three-man body comprised of Curley, Chief Justice Wilfred Bolster of the Municipal Court, and Police Commissioner Eugene C. Hultman. Also present at the hearing was Stanton White, who had just been appointed head of the licensing division, an official title that also carried with it the unofficial role of city censor. The Watch and Ward Society was represented by their president, John Dowling, their legal counsellor, Joseph Crane, and the three "investigators": John Slaymaker, Lester Hills, and Thomas Minton. The hearing was big news:

> Attorney Crane, the Watch and Ward Society counsel, presented the case against the theatre. He had hardly begun when the mayor informed the meeting that he had received a request from David K. Niles, a director of the Civil Liberties committee of Massachusetts, asking permission for a representative of his organization to be present. Judge Bolster commented that with the Watch and Ward present he did not see why the Old Howard did not have a right to be heard, and a secretary of the Mayor called the theatre. Manager Somerby appeared in a few minutes, to be followed by [treasurer] Griffin and counsel Whitman later.
>
> Crane, for the Watch and Ward, declared that he knew of no precedent for having the theatre representative present, but the Mayor smiled genially and said:
>
> "We are creating one now" (*Boston Post*, January 18, 1933).

The *Boston Post* gave the most detailed description among the local papers of what was at times a very amusing proceeding. When the theater representatives arrived, the actual hearing consisted of the eyewitness accounts of Slaymaker, Hills, and Griffin:

> Slaymaker, a dignified little man with gray hair, gray moustache and bone rimmed spectacles . . . proceeded on his report.
>
> The physical conduct of the dances, the "sinuosity of the dancers" were more than suggestive, he said.
>
> The mayor tried to have Slaymaker give more details on the nature of this sinuosity and when the witness said he could not better describe it, the Mayor asked if he could impersonate the dancer for the board's benefit. Slaymaker said he could not.
>
> Investigator Minton then testified. He described Virginia Musio's acts, declaring that she did not hesitate to display a "mobile abdomen."
>
> He termed the show of November 15 as a vicious show and he detailed dialogue between Mike Sachs and Fred Binder to bear his statement out. The Arabian slave market scene figured here in which one buys the top half of the girl and the other buys the lower half. There was voluptuous dancing and disrobing in that show, he said.
>
> The show of December 31st included a Congo moonlight scene with May Joyce and Connie Fanisaw. In this show the audience hissed May Joyce so, because it apparently thought her disrobing act too slow and dull that a policeman had to rush down the aisle and restore order, he said.
>
> The mayor wanted to know if it was a stage policeman. Minton said no, it was one of Commissioner Hultman's policemen.
>
> The mayor asked if it was Commissioner Hultman himself, and both the mayor and the Commissioner had a smile together (*Boston Post*, January 1, 1933).

With the conclusion of the Society's evidence, the management of the Howard was allowed to present its defense. They were aided at times by Curley himself, who at one point said, "At the Old Howard the other day I saw a motion picture called the 'Department Store.' It had more muscle dancing in it than that at the Old Howard show I saw. There was no muscle dancing in any Ann Corio show I saw" (*Boston Post*, January 18, 1933).

Following the conclusion of the defense, the hearing room was cleared and the board deliberated. Within ten minutes it returned with the official finding:

> There has been persistent, flagrant violation. We have neither the right nor the inclination to support the statute standard with one claimed to be more liberal. Those wishing to show or view what some call art, but we call raw filth, must first get the legislature to change the law.
>
> The license is suspended for 30 days beginning January 18, 1933 with the added warning that if on resumption the offense is repeated, the license will be promptly and permanently revoked (*Boston Globe*, January 1933).

Students of Curley say that the Mayor was merely paying lip service to the Society; he was actually a regular patron of the Old Howard. Ann Corio told me that many times during a performance "there would be a commotion in the audience and I'd look down the aisle and there would come Curley and his wife and two men who set up chairs for them in the aisle. He loved the place." After attending a performance at the Howard to, as he put it, "acquaint myself with the type of amusement there," Curley was asked what he thought of the show. "They had a full house," he replied, "but all the people I spoke to seem to come from Maine, New Hampshire and Vermont" (*Boston Post*, January 18, 1933). In his autobiography, Curley talked about closing the Howard:

> I was continually badgered by the eager, lip pursing members of the New England Watch and Ward society, who combined the fervor of bird feeders and disciples of the Anti-Vivisection Society. For some time a group of shocked ladies had been urging me to close the Howard Athenaeum, better known as "The Old Howard."
>
> "I would like to honor your petition," I told the ladies, "but do you realize the historical significance of the Howard Athenaeum? You may think the Howard is well known, but the Old Howard is known in every port of the world. It is one of Boston's great institutions" (*I'd Do It Again*, 1957).

There could be no appeal of the Board's ruling, which was final. The theater closed on January 18, 1933. Business in the lunchrooms, shooting galleries, penny arcades, and hot dog stands in and around the Square fell to disastrous levels. The mayor's office was flooded with protests from people who couldn't understand how, during a depression when work was so scarce, a city could prevent so many from earning a living.

The Howard reopened on February 20. Though the new show's title was "Scrambled Legs," it would be a while before the management could allow things to return to normal. One chorus girl remarked backstage after a rehearsal for the reopening, "We should have brought our red flannels with us" (*American Mercury*, April 1944).

Despite the ever-watchful eye of the Society, the Old Howard eventually returned to its old self — enjoying a naughty reputation, pleasing sailors and mayors alike.

Memories of the Old Howard

For twenty years following the month-long closing, the theater delivered on its promise that there would be "Always something doing from 1 to 11." Although it seems that everybody in the Boston area went to the Howard at some point in their lives, back then no one wanted to admit it — at least not to older family members like mothers and fathers. Some of my favorite interviews were about the Old Howard. Like this one, told by a true Beacon Hill Brahmin:

> My mother was very much Bostonian . . . *very* Bostonian. *Life* magazine was doing a history of four theaters in Boston, and the Howard was one of them. We were all

asked to go down and be in the audience for these pictures that were going to be in the magazine.

My mother got in a taxi and said to the taxi man, "I want to go to 32 Howard Street, please."

So he thought a few minutes and since he knew my mother (because she didn't have a car and took taxis everywhere), he said, "You want to go to the Old Howard, wouldn't you, Mrs. Miller?"

You see, she was very Bostonian and wouldn't say "Old Howard."

Another very proper woman related this tale:

My biggest date was at the Old Howard. My husband came from St. Louis to go to MIT. We met when he was a freshman. And he asked me, "Do you know a place called the Old Howard?"

With that, my mother's face stiffened. You know, *nice* people never went in there, and my mother said, "What are you talking about?"

And this nice young fellow (who eventually became my husband) says he had heard about the place all his life and won't you let Ruth go with me? And my mother replied, "Oh, no decent woman goes to the Old Howard."

[DK: Did you end up going?]

[Laughing] I'm not going to answer you!

Each story from the following trilogy has been repeated so often that they too have become part of the Old Howard's legend.

My old man always told me never to go into the Howard theater because I might see something I wasn't supposed to see. One day I did go in and saw something I shouldn't see — my old man sitting in the front row!

I was in high school, and I snuck into the Howard theater to see an afternoon show, and who do I bump into but my old man! He said, "Your mother better not hear about this."

Have you heard the one about the young prude they forced into going to the Old Howard? They had to drag her in, and then they had to drag her out!

By the thirties the Howard was a legend in the world of show business, growing old but still going strong. A depression and a world war couldn't keep the sailors, businessmen, and students from climbing those stairs on Howard Street to be part of a theatrical legend . . . however tattered the legend was getting.

I was a chemistry major at Northeastern from 1932 to 1937. Back then we used to go to the Old Howard while a chemistry experiment was going on. We'd set up the experiment, take a trolley down to Scollay Square, catch a show at the Howard, then head back and finish the experiment!

What you see today on TV is much more than you saw at the Old Howard back then. The bikinis today are much less than what they stripped to. Back then it was a big deal (Dick Black, former accountant).

I went to school here in Hyde Park, and we'd always skip the last two classes, take the el into town, and see all the shows at the Howard. It was good entertainment as far as we were concerned. There was grace, and they seemed to enjoy doing the show. I remember Ann Corio and Rose la Rose—it was the way they did their act as they strutted across the floor.

The guys back at school were all close-knit, they'd never squeal that you were there. They had a lot of comedians who told really risqué jokes, and the next day we'd all get in a huddle and retell the best ones! (Sammy, still lives in Roslindale).

Going to the Old Howard was always something of a thrill for its patrons, who sometimes saw more than they expected:

It was right after World War II and the Red Sox had been in the World Series and a friend of mine and I went into the Old Howard. Right in the middle of the show when the comedian is doing his thing this fat guy came out of one side of the stage chasing this gorgeous-looking girl. Who was it but Costello of Abbott and Costello. They stopped the show, and the manager came out and introduced them and they reminisced how they had started in burlesque and played the Howard at some point. They were in Boston for the World Series and they decided to come back to their former starting place. They stopped the show, and they did "Who's on First" (Henry).

Abbott and Costello had played the Old Howard when they were starting out in show business. So did Phil Silvers, Milton Berle, Sammy Davis, Jr., and other future radio, movie, and television stars. Red Buttons, although he never played there as an official member of the cast, did perform at the theater:

I did one night at the Howard. I got up on stage, and it was a surprise to my cast and director. I was in town with a pre-Broadway show, *Barefoot Boy with Cheek*, from Max Shulman's book. Nancy Walker and Billy Redfield and I were starring in the show. One night I got them all to go to the Old Howard for a midnight show. And as a special surprise, I walked out with the burlesque comics and I did a couple of sketches.

Almost as famous as some of the acts were some of the men who made up the audience, like the legion of bald-headed men who always occupied the front row. The Harvard boys who occupied the wooden benches in the gallery were said to be fond of throwing spitballs at the bare heads below.

Another audience member that many people recall is a fellow known only as "Clicker Joe." Because he had lost one of his arms in an accident, he couldn't clap his hands. Instead, he carried a small toy which made a clicking sound when pressed. This was his way of applauding.

Bob McKay, now a travel agent, remembers some of the things he saw both on and off the stage:

I used to go to the Old Howard when I was in high school, and it's funny because what you heard about all the bald-headed fellows in the front row was true. Monday morning was the best day to go down there because the censor hadn't shown up yet to see that week's show.

You see ten times more on the beach today than you did onstage back then, and not only that but they had a purple light on the stage so you could barely see what was going on. They used to have comedians, and they were very good. Mike Sachs was blind, and he was better entertainment than some of the girls. I remember one of them, Zorita the Snake Girl.

Back at school everybody knew where you were and the teachers would want a note from your father and you'd make the note up and have a friend sign it.

Mike Sachs was one of the Howard's favorite acts. Blinded by a degenerative eye disease, Sachs had played the Howard so often that after being led onstage by his wife, Alice Kennedy (who also performed there), he could execute his entire routine unassisted, relying only on his memory of the theater. He performed his act so well that many people in the audience left without realizing that the funny man they had just seen was blind.

Mike Monroe, known professionally as "Mr. Tall Top" (for a stilt act he still performs today), used to play the Old Howard with Sachs. He remembers a trick someone played on Sachs one night:

Mike Sachs used to play the piano during his act. Alice, his wife, would put a piece of tape on middle C so when he stepped up to the keyboard he'd know where to start playing. One night somebody moved the tape, and he started to play. It took him a few bars to find his way back to C, and boy was he mad.

Boston-area native Steve Mills was, like Sachs and others, a baggy-pants comic, a name that means exactly what it implies. Many practiced this now lost form of comedy, but few were as funny as Mills. One critic described his face as "a lump of dough left behind by some forgetful baker," adding that, "his timing is incredible . . . he is an absolute master" (*This Was Burlesque*, 1968). The Howard crowd loved him.

Another popular comedian was a man who called himself "Cheese and Crackers." Billy Hagan, aware of the strict Boston censors, needed a way to express exasperation onstage, so he borrowed the old parochial school trick of saying "Cheese and Crackers" instead of "Jesus Christ."

The soon-to-be famous were not just on stage at the Old Howard. According to Jack Lemmon's biographer Don Widener, who spoke to a prep school friend of the Academy Award winner, Lemmon used to attend shows at the Old Howard for a particular reason:

Lemmon asked him to go along on a visit to the Old Howard . . . "It was the thing at the time for boys at Andover to go there and see the girls. It was supposed to make you a man, like smoking a cigarette. Jack said he wanted to watch the comics, which is one of those things a boy says when he means something else and needs an acceptable reason for doing it.

They visited the Old Howard several times and Jack . . . actually did go to see the comics work (*Lemmon: A Biography*, 1975).

Though many men still insist today that they, like Lemmon, went to the Old Howard for the comics, not the strippers, the women who graced the Howard's stage are still remembered with amazing clarity by their fans. According to Joe Savino, who worked at the Old Howard, Zorita the Snake Girl was the biggest draw the Howard ever had. The reason, he said, was simple:

She was unique. She did a striptease with a snake. At one point she would throw the snake over her back, and the snake would slither down her back and eventually disappear. She had a gimmick where the snake would disappear, and of course you know where she had everybody believing that it went!

Savino's claim about Zorita's drawing power is not without proof:

One Saturday night I went to the Crawford House to play my usual Saturday night poker game with Charlie Schultz. Charlie was the stage manager of the Casino and a helluva straight man, too.

Now at one point in the night somebody came by and said that it was snowing out but so what, we didn't pay any attention.

When the game broke up *early Monday morning*, the snow was so bad we couldn't get out of the Crawford House. But I had to get to the Howard for the Monday morning show. It was so cold that they had to bring the horse from the milk wagon into the lobby of the hotel so it wouldn't freeze. So I bundled up, I wrapped my feet up in towels and pulled my head down below my coat collar.

I go out, hunched over, wending my way through Scollay Square. It's below zero and there's fifteen inches of snow. I finally get to Howard Street and I'm walking up the street and *I'm bumping into people!* So I can't figure it out. I finally realized, there must be a line going into the Howard theater two blocks long.

Zorita was the opening attraction that day.

Other strippers come to mind. Lily St. Cyr started her act practically nude and then proceeded to put her clothes back on. Then there was Diane (the Flame of New Orleans) Ross, whose act consisted of a monkey catching the clothes Miss Ross threw across the stage as she disrobed. Walter Winchell found the six-foot, four-inch tall Lois DeFee so striking that he called her the Eiffel Eyeful. But it was DeFee's marriage to a midget that most people remember. That, and the joke that went along with that publicity-inspired union:

Q: How did the midget make love to Lois DeFee?
A: Someone put him up to it.

During the last few years of the Howard, the stage manager was Max Michaels, nicknamed "Smiling Max" by those who worked there because he never seemed to wear anything but a somber expression on his face. Stricter than any city censor, Max knew every joke, every bump, and every grind in the performers' acts. Mondays were set aside for a full rehearsal of the show, which Max would time. Then he'd tell the performers what they could and could not do. According to those who worked there, what Max said was law.

"It was tough, but it was fun," says Barbara English, who remembers her first night as a stripper:

> Sometime during the war a stripper didn't show up for her act, and they said *you* go on, and I said "Oh, what do I know? What do I do?" And this was for a midnight show on the Fourth of July. We had a late rehearsal the night before, and that morning I had gotten up and driven to Falmouth to go to the beach. And I slept. I got so sunburned that I could hardly move, but they said "You *have* to go on" . . . I was like a robot!

Ann Corio had gone "legit" by the 1950s, and although no one ever achieved the special relationship she had with the Howard, many strippers were still able to "pack 'em in the aisles." Georgia Sothern was one such perfomer. She describes her days at the Howard in her autobiography:

> Boston! The Old Howard Theatre. College boys in lines that stretched down the street and overflowed into Scollay Square. Those kids were the greatest! I received flowers by the bushel and they showed up every night in droves, and when I would try to leave the stage door after the last show, it would take an hour before I could get away into a cab and get to my hotel. I loved every minute of our stay at the Howard (*My Life in Burlesque*, 1972).

Ann Corio, one of Sothern's close friends, describes her act:

> Her music, "Hold That Tiger," was wild, the orchestra played at full blast and full tempo, and Georgia came on stage in full flight. And she'd work up momentum. Faster and faster the music would roar, and Georgia would be at the front of the stage, one hand cascading her long red hair over her face, the other outstretched to keep her balance as her hips blurred back and forth at a fantastic tempo. . . . You didn't shout from the audience to Georgia to take it off, there was no time. By the time she was finished, the whole theatre seemed to explode in a sigh. The audience was almost as exhausted watching as Georgia was performing (*This Was Burlesque*, 1968).

During her days on the circuit, Sothern spoke to a reporter about a backstage trick that she and the other more seasoned performers would pull on the newcomers — a trick that worked everywhere but in Boston:

We have a gag we play on the new girls. About half an hour before curtain time we'd start them looking for the key to the curtain, chasing all over the place asking stage-hands and janitors — getting them all excited by telling them they can't go on until the curtain is unlocked. At the Old Howard that gag won't work — they do lock the curtain (*Boston Herald*).

Performing in burlesque was not without its hazards. One fan remembers Sothern in an embarrassing moment onstage:

Way back about 1940 I remember going to see Georgia Sothern. They [the strippers] used to touch themselves up around the nipples, usually with lipstick, so they would be more pronounced through the costume. She had apparently used mercurichrome to make herself all nice and rosy, and the stuff had run down all the way to her stomach by the time she was done with her act.

Although many performers did play the Howard before moving on to the legitimate stage, the story that former actor and President Ronald Reagan played there is not true. This rumor was started when a New England college found an old program with Reagan's name on the bill. He was the star of the movie *That Hagen Girl*, which played between the burlesque shows.

The Candy Butcher

Not all the activity at the Old Howard was confined to the bumps and grinds of the strippers. Every show was also punctuated by the chatter of a salesman unique to the burlesque theater. As soon as the intermission curtain lowered, the candy butcher would appear at the side of the stage, dressed in a mismatched suit and wearing a large diamond pinky ring, which he flashed in the spotlight. His chatter, remembered here by Dan McCole of the *Boston Herald*, is recalled fondly by every sucker who dished out a couple of quarters for what usually turned out to be a box of stale candy. But it was worth it just to hear him speak:

Good even, laze 'n gennemen. Tonight I would like to welcome you to the Old Howard theater, here in the heart of Boston's historic Scollay Square.

Now I realize you're a broad-minded audience, else you would not be present. To-night, laze 'n gennemen, I have a special offer for you — an offer of which you will no doubt say to yourself — "How can they do this? Why, they must be losing money with bargains like this."

In honor of the star of our presentation this evening, "Bubbles La Bomba," who you all saw on this very stage just moments ago, and with her permission, we can offer our specially commissioned photographs of Bubbles in a pose that caused the recent Labor Day riots at the Detroit Blueberry Festival.

This full-sized eight-by-ten photo, suitable for framing for your home, comes coupled with a special magazine which cannot be purchased on the outside. I repeat—and I know you're a broad-minded audience, otherwise you would not be here—this magazine cannot be bought outside this theater. This magazine has many features that can only be described as bizarre, intriguing, and exotic and fun to read in your own home.

Along with this magazine and the picture of our star for the evening, Bubbles La Bomba, we will include a photo of the strongest man in the world—Mr. Charles Atlas.

Now, laze 'n gennemen, I know you're a broad-minded audience—otherwise you wouldn't be here—but if you take the photo of Charles Atlas—a life-sized eight-by-ten—and a photo of the lovely star of this evening's presentation, Miss Bubbles La Bomba, and place them one on top of the other, you can shake them in the dark under your seats and you will see things that will make your hair stand on end. You'll find out why the lights have been flashing on and off in the back rooms at many swanky Beacon Hill homes and men's clubs.

Now you have article number one, the magazine. Article number two, of course, is the photos of the lovely Bubbles and the strongest man in the world Charles Atlas . . . both suitable for framing in your home.

So here we have article number three. Laze 'n gennemen, a plain pair of playing dice. You can take these dice and you can play craps with your friends. You can take these dice and you can play Monopoly with your children in your own homes. However, if you take these dice, placing one against the other in any infinite number of combinations, turning them one side to the other, again and again, and holding them up to the lightbulb, and you will see things that made Errol Flynn blush and giggle in the office of his Hollywood attorney.

Now I know you are a broad-minded audience, elsewise you wouldn't be here. And I know you're saying to yourself, "How can they do this?" Of course we can't sell these items where they would cost twenty to thirty-five dollars. But here is our secret. We do not sell them. No, laze 'n gennemen—we give them to you free. Yes, free. In this world where's there's no free lunch—we give article one, the magazine; article two, the photos which are suitable for framing for your home; and article three, the exotic dice—all free. Free with the delicious candy we are offering tonight.

I know you're a broad-minded audience—otherwise you wouldn't be here. Now, laze 'n gennemen, you say to yourself, "How can they do this, the candy alone must cost fifteen, twenty dollars."

No, laze n' gennemen. Not fifteen or twenty dollars. Not even ten dollars. Not five dollars. No not even one dollar. Each and every one of you can have this complete home entertainment set plus a delicious and healthful candy bar for just fifty cents.

An', laze 'n gennemen, as soon as anyone finds a ten or twenty or a fifty dollar bill in with the delicious candy treat, please hold up the bill so we can all see them. There's a man in the rear holding up a watch—a beautiful Waltham timepiece. Congratulations, sir! And there, over there—there's a man with a—Friend, is that a twenty? No, why it's a fifty—a fifty dollar bill (Dan McCole).

The winners were actually other vendors taking turns waving watches and bills. Some people knew that and most others probably guessed it, but that didn't stop young men from forking over fifty cents and trying desperately to arrange those dice to see the shocking and titillating image.

> They [the candy butchers] had a wonderful patter. That's what seized me, and I remember thinking at one point that patter was as good as the American tobacco auctioneer. It had a kind of a rise and fall to it, and I thought somebody ought to put that kind of thing on the stage and make a song out of it (Carl DeSuze, broadcaster at WBZ for forty-five years).

Joe Savino, the Howard's candy butcher during much of the forties, laughs when he talks about the patter he used to perform:

> It was a total lie from start to finish. But the lies were so outrageous that almost nobody got upset. I used to tell the audience that they would get a very fine cowhide wallet and it was nothing but a paper wallet . . . you could buy it for four cents in any novelty store.

Savino remembers that the performers were rarely friends with the candy butchers "because they felt we were degrading the burlesque theater and the burlesque actor. Besides, we made more money than them!"

Jack Rosen was a candy butcher in 1950 when he was interviewed by *Colliers* magazine for a story they did on the Old Howard. Rosen, in retrospect, was a little less than candid about his job:

> Mr. Somerby insists that we talk for only six minutes at each appearance. Up here in Boston we never resort to such old Burlesque tricks as turning up the heat to sell more drinks or ice cream on a slow night. Boston audiences are very high class. We don't insult their intelligence (*Colliers*, September 30, 1950).

That may or may not have been true, but the sentiment certainly didn't apply to youngsters starting out in the candy-selling game. Leo Ajemian, who eventually went on to manage other theaters in Boston, remembers his first week on the job as a candy butcher at the Old Howard:

> When I started they really put me through the hurdles. They'd give me a big box of candy, and I made the mistake of not counting it. I'd go out and I'd be selling the candy and I'd come back and they'd say, "Hey, you owe us another five or ten dollars." They were shortchanging me, and at the end of the week I ended up owing them money. I caught on to that and became an usher.

The Last Days of the Howard

Al Somerby was the general manager of the Howard for its last twenty years. He bought out the Lothrop family's interest in the theater in 1935. Five years later he bought the building and became the sole owner and operator of what was for many years the most profitable burlesque house in the country. "It's the poor man's musical comedy," he said. "Burlesque will always be with us." Somerby once claimed that the expression "They were hanging from the rafters" was born at the Old Howard (*Colliers*, September 30, 1950).

Responding to the still vigilant cries of citizens in the Watch and Ward Society who claimed burlesque contributed to crime, he said, "I wouldn't be in this business another minute if I believed that. I have six kids of my own, you know. The people in our business are the finest, cleanest folks I know. Their conduct is exemplary and I resent the slurs cast their way by those who criticize without knowing all the facts" (*Colliers*, September 30, 1950).

Getting all the facts on the Howard was not always an easy task for city censors. It is a well-known fact that the ticket taker at the Howard was hired not for his ticket tearing ability but for his knowledge of building inspectors, police officers, and erstwhile censors. Spotting one of them approaching the box office, he would drop his foot onto a button planted in the floor. This activated a light placed among the footlights which would flash on and off, warning those onstage that, in Howard parlance, the "house was down" and they should edit their act.

This cat and mouse game continued for years with the Howard, ever vigilant, always winning. But in October of 1953 the game was finally lost. James McCarthy, now assistant commissioner for Elderly Affairs in Boston, was on the vice squad and tells what happened:

> There was a complaint from a church group or maybe the Watch and Ward Society. What happened was we went in and gathered evidence and presented it to the Chief Justice of the Municipal Court. We brought a sixteen-millimeter camera into the theater without them knowing it. Bernie Hurley took the actual film. We arrested the manager, the assistant manager, and the participants in the show: Rose La Rose, Irma the Body, and Princess Domain. There weren't too many people in the theater.
>
> It was kinda funny the day we presented the case in court. Chief Justice Elijah Adlow of the Municipal Court looked out in the courtroom, and it was jam-packed, and says, "We should have charged admission."
>
> Judge Adlow said at one point, "You know, I was in the Old Howard many times. Maybe I'm responsible for the Old Howard, too."

At the same time, a three-man board, much like the one that had closed the Howard twenty years before, was also meeting to decide if the theater should close. Acting Mayor Francis X. Ahern, the city council president who took control when Mayor John Hynes left on a three-week trip, was quoted as saying: "I positively will not tolerate any filthy or indecent shows in our city. Any further complaints of this nature will be met with the most drastic and summary action while I am acting Mayor" (*Boston Globe*, October 31, 1953).

The threatened closing was not headline news, as it had been in 1933. The hearing also lacked a certain style, probably because there was no Mayor Curley to liven up the proceedings. It did have its moments, though:

Whoever said Justice is blind should have been in Boston's Municipal Court yesterday. On trial — with movie exhibits — were three strip teasers and three art impresarios.

At the bench was Elijah Adlow. The courtroom was filled to capacity — and as attentive as the Old Howard's famed "row of bald headed men."

. . . Miss Goodneighbor [Irma the Body], who described her act as "an interpretive dance depicting the All-American girl," sipped a bottle of milk during one part of the hearing.

"I come out wearing a stole, 35 pounds of beads, a hoop and 65 yards of orchard tulle," she explained to a hushed courtroom. "My outfit weighs forty pounds."

Judge Adlow expressed curiosity about the disrobing part of the act. "I am always covered within the law," she said.

. . . Later, when a witness for the defense insisted there was nothing immoral in the costuming and the acts, Judge Adlow asked: "Do they ever vary the monotony by wearing overcoats?" (*Boston Globe*, November 8, 1953).

During the week that the case was being heard in court, Acting Mayor Ahern discussed the fate of the Old Howard with the censorship board. Fans, hoping to sway the outcome of those deliberations, spoke out in the papers with letters to the editor:

To the Editor of the *Boston Herald*:

As a true devotee of the arts I am a constant reader of your superior reviews of Boston's artistic activities. However, ennui engulfs my jaded palate as I peruse the usual well-conceived but somehow dull and bourgeois critiques of the Symphonym, the Theatre Guild, etc. . . . It is only when my eyes light upon the alas! sporadic reviews of the current fare for the gods billed at the Old Howard that life again seems worth living — the appetite whetted, the intellect piqued. One realizes again that the truly analytical mind, the cultivated approach to true criticism of the arts has not vanished from the contemporary scene. Congratulations to the authors of these exquisite vignettes!

Frieda Nichols
Marblehead

(*Boston Herald*, November 3, 1953)

Dear Sirs,

Burlesque in Boston is in danger and I wish to speak in its defense. Since the arrest of the three Queens I have scanned newspapers for one favorable item on this little sister of the musical comedy. I have found none. Instead the District Attorney's action makes my blood boil until it vaporizes and forms an angry red cloud over my head threatening to do more harm to my peace of mind and morals than all the Burlesque shows in the world.

If the District Attorney wishes to do things for the morals of his charges let him pay considered attention to many items in our daily papers. This La Rosa business; far more dangerous to public morals than the Rose La Rose affair. Think of the citizens reading all about the alleged attempts of a successful young man to become married to a young woman already married and to a Korean Vet, too. This strikes at the very foundations of our society, much more so than a little rowdy comedy and the flash of bare limbs.

He says that Boston has a youth problem. Of course, it always has, and always will have, and the current upsurge of it is not stemming from the junction of Howard, Hanover, and Tremont. It is stemming from the constant tide of blood and violence that flows from every crime program on TV and radio. Add to the volume of audio and video blood, lust, avarice, rape, and licentiousness; that of the pulp, pocketbook, and comic magazines and you have the answer to our juvenile problem. In all the time that I have been attending burlesque performances, and that is 18 years and includes several cities, I have never seen one act that advocated death or injury by violence.

Burlesque is an old and respected art, for accuracy's sake, we can call it a folk art. It can be traced back to Aristophanes who, around 430 BC, satirized people and their tragedies, and is the natural way for an intellectually free people to poke fun at the things that disturb, amaze, injure or boss them.

This whole thing smacks of censorship and I don't want to see them do it.

If investigation shows the need of a restraining hand on burlesque let it be done but as far as that goes I am perfectly willing to leave the whole matter in the hands of our censor.

If the authorities feel the need of more guidance for our youth make the presentation of birth certificates at the burlesque box office mandatory for those of doubtful age.

Herbert Ross
Mattapan

(*Boston Herald*, November 5, 1953)

Alas, this impassioned prose did little to change the outcome of either proceeding. On November 9, 1953, the Boston Board of Censorship suspended performances at the Howard and the Casino Theatre, also located in Scollay Square. A week earlier the municipal court found the three strippers guilty of performing a lewd and immoral show and fined them each two hundred dollars. After handing down his sentence, Judge Adlow bemoaned the fact that "a girl has to throw her hip out of joint to get a hand from a Boston audience" (*Boston Globe*, November 1, 1953).

The fines were appealed, but the restoration of the Howard's license was never pursued. Many say that a sagging box office made the closing inevitable, especially since the owners also ran the Casino Theatre on Hanover Street, which by that time had outpaced the Old Howard's ticket sales. America's oldest theater was closed and would stay that way.

The Howard remained empty for eight years (save for the occasional vagrant who used it as sleeping quarters) while plans for a new Government Center were being drawn up by the city. A private office building, called Center Plaza, was to stretch along Cambridge Street on the site of what used to be Tremont Row, where many of Scollay Square's other landmarks were located. Its northernmost section would lie where the Old Howard was. Ann Corio tells what happened next:

> In 1959 the Howard National Theatre and Museum Committee was organized to save the theatre from threatened demolition. The committee wanted to convert the Old Howard into a national shrine where operas and plays could be presented.
> In 1961 I arrived in Boston with the first edition of our show "This Was Burlesque." We were going to try it out in a nightclub in the vicinity. I hastened right over to pay a visit to be my beloved Old Howard, even though it was empty. Then, a few weeks later, a mysterious fire started in the theatre and swept through the whole interior. Only the charred outside shell remained standing (*This Was Burlesque*, 1968).

The three-alarm blaze started somewhere in the roof structure about noon on June 20, 1961, and spread rapidly. Except for a few vagrants, all of whom escaped, there was no one inside. Fireman Ed Lowney was the only person injured. Although the official fire department report reads, "This fire is of undetermined origin," many fans and those close to the Museum Committee expressed skepticism. Dean Gitter, head of the restoration group, was quite firm that day when he spoke to reporters after the fire:

> It seems incredible that at the precise moment when, over protests from some quarters, its [the theatre's] restoration was nearly assured that it should finally succumb to accidental holocaust.
> It is also unfortunate that within hours of the fire's discovery the building commissioner, allegedly fearing for the public safety, had a wrecking crew on this site whose steel ball quickly accomplished what the fire had failed to do.
> Although the four stone walls were virtually intact the building department denied the request of the committee that the walls be left standing for a mere 24 hours, with the area cordoned off, until the committee could engage a contractor to shore up the remains (*Boston Globe*, June 21, 1961).

Most of the granite facade was torn down that day, leaving little for the restoration committee to work with, and so the idea for a national museum in Boston was abandoned. The Howard had one more bow to take, however, as Ann Corio describes:

> I went right there after the fire and looked brokenhearted at the ruins. Then I saw an amazing sight. It was as if that old burnt-down theatre was saying its own personal goodbye to one star on hand for the funeral. The raging fire had burned through layers and layers of posters on its walls — all the way through to a poster put up twenty years before. That poster was of me (*This Was Burlesque*, 1968).

The wake of the Old Howard, June 20, 1961. The bald-headed men came to pay their last respects (From the collection of Irene Shwachman).

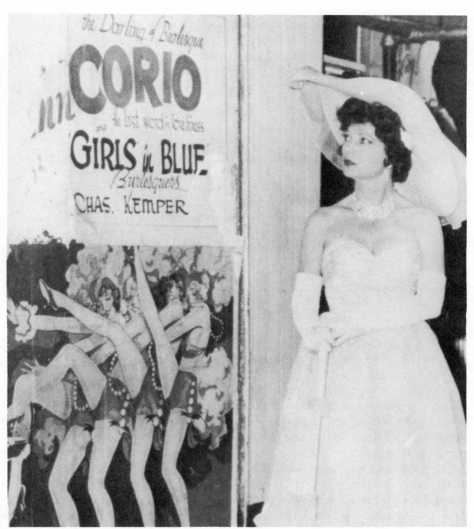

After the fire at the Old Howard, Ann Corio came to pay her last respects, too. She found that the blaze had spared this poster of a show she had performed almost twenty years before (Courtesy of Ann Corio, *This Was Burlesque*, 1968).

The demise of the Old Howard was a source of great sadness for many people. Francis W. Hatch, Harvard class of 1919 and a theatrical history scholar, was moved to write this tribute in song:

> Some coward
> Closed the Old Howard.
> They're hanging crepe on Scollay Square.
>
> World tension
> Makes this suspension
> Almost more than we can bear.
>
> What's become of Flo LaVerne and Peaches de la Rose?
> Brooding with the unemployed, wearing all their clothes?
>
> Some dastard
> Went ahead and plastered
> A sheriff's notice on the door.
>
> Some coward
> Closed the Old Howard.
> We don't have Burley anymore!

Today there are precious few reminders of the Old Howard left in Government Center. A plaque was placed on the location of the stage (a concrete bench behind One Center Plaza), and dedicated on October 28, 1968, by a group of Harvard alumni led by Allan Schulte and Robert Lingley. A visit to the site shows just how precious land is within the area. There is barely enough room for a few benches stuck between One Center Plaza and the courthouse.

Boston's attempt to create a replacement for Scollay Square and the Old Howard, in what was officially designated an "adult entertainment zone," ultimately failed. The Pilgrim Theatre on Washington Street came closest to the Howard in spirit. Opened in the early seventies by former Howard candy butcher Joe Savino it attempted, at first, to present a complete burlesque bill of fare, complete with baggy-pants comedians. But the times had changed and the theater ended up, like the rest of the so-called Combat Zone, with uninspired nude dancing and X-rated movies.

Francis Hatch was right—we don't have Burley anymore. And if the warm smiles of those who remember the days of Ann and Georgia and Peaches are any indication, then we are missing something special today. To understand the difference between what passes today for racy entertainment and what was performed at the Howard, think of the difference between radio and TV. The Howard was like radio. In pre-TV days, radio listeners had to imagine faraway places and visualize the action taking place there. A trip to the Howard also required something of an imagination, for there was no real nudity . . . only flashes of what you *thought* might be a part of the stripper's anatomy. Today, as in television, nothing is left to the imagination. Patrons of strip joints are no longer participants in the act, they are merely paying customers. When the tease went out of strip so did the fun. Is it any wonder that when both performers and patrons remember the Old Howard they smile?

CHAPTER

5

The Sailors

Soon after moving to Boston in 1981, I returned home to New York for Thanksgiving with my family. In attendance that year was my uncle, who had been a medical doctor on board a destroyer during World War II. We proceeded to reenact a conversation that has probably taken place for years in homes across America.

"So you're in Boston now," my uncle began. "How are things in Scollay Square?"

"I don't know, I've never heard of the place," I replied. "What's Scollay Square?" And so my uncle told me my first Scollay Square story:

I was a doctor in the navy and when the ship used to pull into port [Charlestown], the commanding officer would get on the intercom and give his shore leave speech. "Men," he'd say, "It's liberty time in Boston and you've earned it. Just remember the rules, and rule number-one is, Don't go to Scollay Square."

So where do you suppose was the first place all those kids went? Scollay Square, of course! So I spent the rest of *my* shore leave patching up the guys who went to Scollay Square!

Although servicemen from other branches of the armed forces used to go there, sailors were primarily responsible for keeping the Square and its many bars and tattoo parlors busy. This had been true since the 1800s, but it was during World War II that the Square really gained its notorious reputation as a sailors' hangout. The Charlestown Navy Yard, where many Allied ships came for repairs and supplies, was located just across Boston Harbor from Scollay Square, twelve minutes away by subway. Boston historian George Weston explains:

During the war years the much maligned square lived by, and for, the boys of the Navy. Its restaurants, stores, bars and other services were keyed to the tastes of the Navy personnel. Lunchrooms offered the toothsome hot dog, the nutritious hamburger, and the succulent submarine. Prices were low and the places were reasonably clean although unreasonably noisy.

Photo studios enabled Jack to secure a lasting memento of the current girlfriend, or vice versa. Tattoo studios catered to that strange artistic longing which seems at times to attack all men associated with salt water. The artists of the needle would execute any design from a simple cross to a "bird's eye view of Sydney." They advised against girls names. A tattoo is apt to outlive a light o'love, and it was highly embarrassing for a sailor to contemplate matrimony with Helen in his heart and Tessie on his torso. Explanation was required. It was far wiser to have a simple wreath and the word "Mother." That is a love which changeth not (*Boston Ways: High, By and Folk*, 1957).

"Sailor's Haven" and "Boston's Barbary Coast" were two of the more popular nicknames given to Scollay Square. Jim, a navy veteran who prowled the Square during the war, tells why he thinks the area was so popular. His reasons probably apply as much to those who served in World War II as they do to the sailors who came here to relax during the Spanish-American War:

You had young guys who had never been away from home. At eighteen or nineteen they get sent away and they fight. Now they come home on shore leave and they've got money in their pockets and they're not kids anymore.

They've fought a war. The women are available for a small part of the money they got, so why not? A lot of them got drunk for the first time, too. Good thing the MPs were bigger than they were.

The SPs (Shore Patrol) and MPs (Military Police) were soon as much a fixture in Scollay Square as the Steaming Kettle. Eddie, an entertainer in that part of town, recalls:

Above the Red Hat and many other bars, there were rooms where the hookers would go with the clients. Although the police looked the other way, the SPs and MPs would not. If there was a serviceman involved the cops might want to look the other way since there were fighting men involved. But the MPs and SPs did their job.

I might be making it out to be a rougher place than it was. The kind of activity did not involve innocent bystanders, nor were there muggings and rapes. The crime, if that's what you want to call it, was serviceman against serviceman, perhaps a knifing or a fist fight after too much booze.

The Hotel Imperial was the center — forget about the Old Howard — the Hotel Imperial was the center of all the action as far as the soldiers and sailors were concerned. There were three bands playing at the same time within hearing distance of each other. A country western band, our quartet, and when you walked in the door there

No sailor ever complained of a lack of things to do in Scollay Square. This block of buildings along Cambridge Street, in a photo taken around the time of World War II, was just around the corner from the Old Howard (Courtesy of Joe Flashman).

was a band playing downstairs that was mixed, black and white, which was kind of novel because there weren't any such bands anyplace else.

The hotel had two stories and the second floor was open in the middle to the first floor. Every once in a while some sailor or soldier would get drunk and throw another guy off the second floor to the first. The MPs and SPs would rush in. Scollay Square was full of them since the Square was full of servicemen.

Others recalled:

I talked to one SP in the area during the war, and I asked him, "How did you make it?" He told me he would stand outside and let the fight wear itself out and then he would pick them up and take them to the guardhouse (Mike I.).

There was a USO nearby. If the sailors or soldiers bothered a girl walking near the USO then the 4F'ers [civilians exempted from military service] used to beat them up . . . it's true . . . I saw it happen many times. There was a place called the Riverside [near Charles Circle in the West End, not far from the Square], and if a soldier or sailor walked by there and looked at any of the girls that lived around there they'd get beat up. I used to get mad and feel bad because my brother was in the service and I'd wonder if where he was they were beating him up (Mary, a former West Ender).

When some citizens began to worry out loud about the activities of all those servicemen, Police Captain Frank Tiernan of the old Joy Street police station came to their defense. He once went before the city council and told them how, during wartime, over ten thousand servicemen would hit the Square in a week, "and not one ever accosted a girl or was charged with a sex offense" (*Boston Record American*).

Scollay Square's reputation seemed to follow the Navy no matter how far its men traveled:

I was in the navy during World War II, and around the fleet the word was, If you're in Boston go to Scollay Square and be sure to go to Joe & Nemo's. There was the Tattoo Mart where a lot of guys got tattoos. I was in the South Pacific but any guys who were going to Boston would ask me, "How do you get to Scollay Square?" (Bill, who served on a destroyer).

Stories have been passed along claiming that ships sometimes passed each other during patrol in the Atlantic, flashing the message, "How are things in Scollay Square?"

When they finally made it to their favorite port of call, there were usually three things on the sailors' agenda. To begin with, they had been at sea for many lonely months:

When I worked at the Crawford House it was wartime and it was really jumping. And the sailors used to like to have a girl out for a good time and all that stuff. Naturally I was older than a lot of them, so they used to ask me, "Who's a nice girl? Who's nice?" I said, "Its up to you to find out. Spend your money here. You'll have to spend plenty of money to get these girls" (Lucy L., from the West End Branch of the Boston Public Library Collection).

I remember one day these young sailors come flying up to the top of the subway stairs and stop, panting for breath because of the run up from the subway, standing there looking around the Square and saying "Jesus H. Christ, there's nothing here!" I don't know what they expected . . . naked women lying in the street awaiting their arrival? (Paul Chivanne).

Jack's Joke Shop sold more rubber goods than anyplace else in Boston. Many of the sailors would take their dates after the show and buy some rubber goods and take them to a hotel room. [He meant condoms, not rubber chickens.] (Ralph Saya).

Sailors were thirsty, too. Ida Kaplan worked the bars in Scollay Square during the war and remembers her customers very well:

When they had money they were pretty good tippers. The army would never tip, they were pretty cheap. When the sailors were broke, we used to know. When four or five sailors would come in from a ship and order beers they'd give me fifty cents, or else they'd say "Ida, I'm broke" so I'd buy them fifty-cent beers because I got to know them when the ships were in. So when they got money they would put it on the table and say, "Ida, help yourself out to tips." They would sometimes bring in gifts to trade for beer or try and sell a watch they were wearing for a few dollars. Then when they had the money they'd come back and buy the watch back for an extra dollar. But I wasn't out for the money because I had a brother who was in the service.

And of course, there were the tattoo parlors. Henry, like a lot of young men on leave, found himself at Dad's Tattoo Parlor near the Old Howard:

Outside were all the designs that you could chose from. I chose this design. It's called "Death Before Dishonor." It's the dagger with the snake. I was seventeen, and it cost only five dollars. It hurt like hell.

First, they washed your arm with alcohol. Then they'd use tracing paper and draw the outline of the drawing on your arm with a machine that had a needle going up and down a few times each second. Then they'd fill in the colors with another needle. The whole thing took less than an hour.

It hurt so much but they didn't give you anything for it, so the sailors and the college kids used to get drunk so they'd be immune to the pain. Me, I was too young to get drunk but I could get a tattoo.

Most sailors, of course, managed to do both. This priceless story from a former swabbie now living in South Carolina is good evidence that drinking and getting tattooed don't mix:

During the war my ship came in to Boston, and me and some of my shipmates went to Scollay Square. Well, I got really looped and the next thing I remember I'm back in my bunk on board with this searing pain on my buttocks! I mean it was like fire . . . I didn't know if I was cut up or what. So I turned to a bunkmate of mine and asked him to take a look, and I asked him, "Am I bleeding?" "No," he says, "but you've got a tattoo of a pink elephant on your left cheek!" And it's been there ever since, my small reminder of Scollay Square.

The sailors, especially those from small towns, were sometimes the targets of con men. Mary lived in the West End and tells about one particular man who had a very polished act:

There was this character in Scollay Square — what a faker he was! He used to get out in the street when the sailors went by and all he needed was a net. He'd drag them in. My sister would have me going down there maybe two times a week. He'd send me on errands to fix the watches and rings. He'd cheat the sailors and tell them it was this big diamond ring, or he'd get hot stuff. He'd say, "Look! Look how beautiful it looks on her fingers." He'd have me put my finger out and of course I'd have nice young fingers, and he'd say "See how beautiful. Take it. Take it. Take it!" Then he'd fake enough people and one of them would come back, so he'd run out the back door and he'd tell me to say, "I don't know where the boss is, I can't touch the register." That used to scare me (West End Boston Public Library Collection).

Most of the soldiers and sailors who prowled Scollay Square during the war were not Boston area residents. One ex-swabbie put it this way: "The hometown boys usually skipped Scollay Square. They had done everything there was to do in the Square when they had hooked high school, which for many wasn't that long ago."

Some called Scollay Square (shown here just after the war) a "Sailor's Haven," others labeled it "Boston's Barbary Coast." (Courtesy of the Bostonian Society/Old State House).

Another brand of sailor, often overlooked, was the Merchant Marine. The container ships they traveled on, dubbed "Liberty Ships," were so crudely made that more than half never made it across the Atlantic. A popular phrase among the seamen was "Give me death, but not a Liberty Ship!" That's what makes this story, told by long-time Boston resident Barney Stone, all the more poignant:

I had a friend who was an attorney, and his office was over the Suffolk County Savings Bank [at the corner of Scollay Square and Pemberton Street]. This was a very dignified, very quiet attorney, and he tells me this story:

It's during the war, 1943 or 1944, and a sea captain comes in and introduces himself and says, "I have a run from Boston to Murmansk in Russia, and every trip is my last trip. I've been doing this ten, fifteen, times, and when I was in Boston I met this young lady and while they were loading up the ship I lived with her for two, three, weeks at a time. She was the best girl I ever had all over the world. She was terrific."

So the lawyer says, "What do you want me to do?"

"Well, I have a problem. Last night in the room I woke up and found her going through my pockets taking my money. 'What are you doing?' I asked her. 'Well, I'm a hooker she says.' 'You are a hooker?' I said. 'Yes, and I was gonna take some money from you.' 'Well, why didn't you ask me, I would have given you anything you wanted. You were the greatest lady I ever met.' "

So the lawyer says, "What do you want me to do about it?"

So the captain takes out four or five bank books from Boston banks and says, "I'm going to give you authorization, and I want you to find this lady." And he gave him the address. "I want you to bring her in here and please take care of her."

The lawyer says, "What are you doing? You don't owe her anything."

"Oh no," the captain says. "I want you to make sure she gets the money . . . she was the greatest thing I ever found in the world."

The surrender of Japan would signal the beginning of the end of Scollay Square, for without the homesick sailor to spend his time and money in the bars and restaurants, there were precious few customers to keep these businesses open. But on August 15, 1945, nobody really thought about that. They were too busy celebrating America's victory in World War II. Billie Lee remembers one of her favorite days ever:

Well, the Bowdoin Square Theatre is the first place where I worked when I started as a waitress. Then I started being a waitress, a bouncer, and an entertainer and a cook. That was in the forties. I worked there for almost five years. The war was on; there was nothing but sailors. Sailors all over the place. That's all you saw. I worked there when the war ended — VJ Day. God, I didn't think I'd have any clothes on me the way they grabbed a hold of me. Christ, they were pinning purple hearts on me and God knows what else. Oh it was really something! It was beautiful (West End Boston Public Library Collection).

The *Boston Post* reported that:

One of the largest impromptu parades in the city was led by a group of sailors who "invaded" the Crawford House in Scollay Square, "borrowed" an American flag from the stage and gathered thousands of servicemen and civilians and paraded them for nearly two hours through the busy thoroughfares in the North and West Ends.

Starting off with only a flag and a line of 20, the sailors had amassed a "fleet" of nearly 300 even before they stepped from the doors of the restaurant. Within 20 minutes the parade line had been swelled to 1000 as the group marched smartly through Scollay Square to Hanover St., up Washington St. to Brattle St. and then wended its way back to the square.

Not satisfied with the short route the sailors started towards Bowdoin Sq. and gathered nearly 1000 more marchers. Through the side streets off Cambridge St. the parade marched and by the time it reached Scollay Square again police estimated it had a parade line as large as most regular parades seen in Boston during the war years (*Boston Post*, August 16, 1945).

On November 10, 1945, General Dwight D. Eisenhower, the Supreme Allied Commander for the Forces in Europe, was given a parade through Boston. At one point the procession took him up Hanover Street into Scollay Square (how appropriate, after so many thousands of his troops made it their wartime home away from home, that he finally made the same trip). Inspired by his visit, the Women's City Club suggested changing the name of Scollay Square to Eisenhower Square as a way to help restore it to past glories. The idea never made it past the talking stage.

The Charlestown Navy Yard continued to operate during the fifties but at a dramatically scaled down pace, as American military strategists concentrated on air power. By the time the navy regained its place in national defense planning during the sixties, Scollay Square was gone and thousands of sailors were left with only a faded memory or a pink elephant to remind them of their wartime watering hole.

CHAPTER

6

The Crawford House
and Sally Keith

The music began slowly at first, a drumbeat pounding out a jazzy rhythm, while onstage an attractive blonde, wearing a beautifully beaded costume, moved seductively to the sound of the drums. Dangling from each of her breasts was a tassel about eight inches long.

The wartime audience, made up of businessmen, sailors, husbands, wives, and young men with their dates, stopped talking. Waitresses continued to move about the crowd serving drinks, but the room was so quiet that, when the drums momentarily stopped, one could almost hear the tassels beginning to sway in the nightclub air.

Suddenly the blonde's left shoulder twitched and a tassel began to move, slowly at first, around in a circle. The drumbeat continued to pound out its tempo when her other shoulder twitched and the tassel on her other breast began to twirl—in the opposite direction! Both tassels were going faster now, each in opposite directions, spinning furiously like airplane propellers.

The audience had, by this time, begun to applaud and holler with appreciation . . . but she wasn't done yet. As the trumpet and piano started to play, she turned around and the audience could see that attached to her costume, on her posterior, were two more tassels *both spinning in opposite directions!*

This was the act of the famed Sally Keith, who was known the world over as the "Queen of the Tassels" from the late 1930s to the early 1950s. When people speak about Scollay Square, the landmarks most often mentioned are the Howard theater, Joe & Nemo's hot dogs, and Sally Keith.

There's no doubt about it. Her act made a lasting impression on anyone who saw her perform. "San Francisco had its Golden Gate Bridge, Chicago its Loop, and New York its Empire State Building, but Boston had Sally Keith — better built and more fun to look at than any of those other monuments!" someone once said. Fans, like this one, still recall her act:

> First-year medical students at a certain university in Boston would be taken to the Crawford House by their professor for the purpose of seeing Sally Keith. The next day he would give them a test on what muscles she used in her tassel act!

A very proper blue-blooded woman who still lives on Beacon Hill (and who made me promise not to use her name) told this story:

> It was the Crawford House where we used to go. I worked for the government and my husband worked on newspaper row and we would get together and go down to the Crawford House where Sally Keith would perform. She appeared in a very scant costume, but I suppose today it wouldn't seem so scant. She could make her tassels — oh, my I shouldn't be saying this to you — well she made the tassels on her breasts move in opposite directions [giggling now]. Don't tell anyone I said this! She was an institution down there . . . I mean that's why we went!

The Crawford House itself was something of a historical treasure to Boston as well. Originally a hotel on Brattle Street when built in 1848, it boasted the first passenger elevator in this country as well as a high-caliber clientele. Massachusetts Senator Daniel Webster stayed there on his visits to Boston, as did other dignitaries.

In 1860 the Crawford House bought and tore down the Minoken Oyster House at the head of Brattle Street so that it could expand. For many years a bank did business on the first floor of the hotel. The dining room was one of Boston's more popular restaurants and was, up until the twenties, the home of some rather quaint traditions, as we learn from a former West Ender:

> I used to be taken to tea at the Crawford House when I was very young. This was about 1914, and I'd be all dressed up in my Mary Janes as a little girl. My father was a doctor at the Massachusetts General Hospital and we'd get taken in to see him and have tea at the Crawford House.

In 1919 Prohibition became law, and the Crawford House was no longer allowed to sell liquor. For many people, alcohol had been the main reason for eating out. Business began to decline. By offering a show during dinner, the Crawford House, like so many other restaurants also feeling the pinch, hoped to bring in a steady flow of customers. At first the shows consisted of singers and dancers. These were followed by comedians, jugglers, and magicians, all of whom helped the Crawford House survive the liquor-less twenties. When Prohibition was repealed, the Crawford House continued presenting shows in its nightclub. But without exception, no show at the Crawford House was ever as popular as Sally Keith's. When she performed there was rarely an empty seat. When she was off or booked elsewhere, it usually meant a bad night's business, not only for the Crawford House but for the rest of the Square as well.

Like Ann Corio, who had brought women to the Old Howard and to burlesque shows, Sally also drew large numbers of women. Many came out of curiosity, others out of admiration or awe. Just how *did* she do that, many of them wondered. One former female patron reported:

> I would have made a million bucks with a tassel concession in the Ladies Room at the Crawford House. During intermission I'd go in to powder my nose, and I'd see all the women standing in front of the mirror trying to make themselves go in opposite directions! I could have made a million!

Dick Sinnot, who was head of the city licensing board (and therefore Boston's de facto city censor) during part of Sally's reign, jokes about the reason her show was never banned:

> I always thought there was a conspiracy between the city censors that came before me and chiropractors. You see, a lot of husbands would take their wives to the Crawford House to see Sally Keith, and later that night when the women got home they'd try and do the tassel number and throw their backs out!

Fellow performer and emcee Eddie Baker remembers audience members "taking bets on which tassel would stop first, the right one or the left!"

Sally Keith grew up near Chicago, where her father was a policeman. At the age of fourteen she changed her last name from Katz to Keith and began performing as a dancer. The tassel act followed when Sally was in her late teens. Her mother kept a close eye on Sally and was often seen backstage supervising the constant flow of men who wanted to meet the Tassel Queen. The people who knew Sally best, among them agents and fellow performers, remember her as a bright, funny woman who never took herself or her act too seriously. Timmy Goldberg, a member of the comedy group The Nuts Brothers, remembers his days with Sally fondly:

> When I worked with Sally Keith I used to do a takeoff on her before she went on. I used to do the tassels just the way she did them. I used to make them go both ways and up and down. And you know who gave me those tassels? She did. She was a great gal.

Carl DeSuze, who was a fixture on Boston radio for almost half a century, remem-

The Crawford House as it looked during Prohibition (Courtesy of the Bostonian Society/Old State House).

bers interviewing Sally for a remote broadcast from the Crawford House during the war:

> I interviewed Sally Keith for WBZ, and I remember she tried very hard to come off tough and nonchalant about herself. Off the air she made it a point to say, "I put aside a bunch of my money for war bonds — I have these boys in mind when I go onstage and make an ass of myself!"

Sally was very well paid for her act — about six hundred dollars a week plus free room and board at the Crawford House. This left her with a lot of spending money. Ethel "Ettie" McKay was an agent who booked many of the acts that used to play Scollay Square, and over the years she developed a friendship with Sally. McKay recalled that one of Sally's purchases made quite an impression:

> Sally Keith didn't drive, you know, but she made a lot of money and she wanted a car that would match her blond hair. So she went out and bought this yellow Cadillac, which she couldn't drive. So whenever she came to town I'd drive her around town from show to show in this big yellow Cadillac. What a sight we made!

One of Mayor Curley's sons, a priest at a North End parish, was part of an amusing incident involving Sally Keith. The church had decided to hold a rummage sale and auction. Sally wanted to do her part, so she donated a pair of her tassels. A slightly flustered but patient Father Curley had to turn down the gift tactfully. After all, it would probably have raised more than all the other items combined, and the good father did not want to have to explain to the diocese just how he had raised so much money.

The Sultan of Scollay Square

A young man named Alan Schwartz managed the Crawford House. His father, Harry, was a very successful entrepreneur, who at one time owned the American House, the Rialto Theatre, the Crawford House, and various other smaller establishments, including tattoo parlors and photography stores in the Square. When Harry died at the age of forty-five in 1936, Alan, a freshman at Brown University, came home to take care of the family business.

Alan Schwartz fulfilled his family's wishes and ran the Crawford House until it was torn down by the city in 1962. He was well liked and respected by performers and staff who, quite understandably, may have been initially a bit wary of a twenty-year-old trying to run a business in Scollay Square. Alan surprised them with his abilities. So much so that when he was drafted in 1943, the whole Square turned out for a going-away party that is still remembered as one of the best ever by those lucky enough to have been invited.

Aside from his managerial skills, Alan's reputation as a playboy is legendary. Handsome and well built, he was constantly seen with the prettiest chorus girls. His "ladies' man" status was sealed in 1942, when *Boston Globe* columnist Vern Miller dubbed Alan the "Sultan of Scollay Square." Dr. Henry Kaplan, who worked his way through Harvard medical school as the Crawford House night manager, remembers that his duties exceeded the administrative:

> I would also keep Alan's girlfriends separated. Alan lived in the Crawford House, and his girlfriend at the time was the captain of the line named Julie. He'd have a lot of girls and when they'd call I'd say, "Well, Mr. Schwartz is in conference." Alan once said to me, "I'll take care of the girls, you take care of the studies."

A Boston Hot Spot

From behind the front desk Henry Kaplan saw one of the most exciting places in Boston during the war: the lobby of the Crawford House. Here the entertainers and the agents, the politicians and ward bosses, the bookies and burlesque queens, would gather to talk, argue, make deals, fight, or show off new routines. Officials and military men of the Allied forces, who were glimpsing Boston's lighter side, also passed through.

Later in the evening the hotel would entertain the "tuxedo crowd." These were large groups who had been to nightclubs such as the Coconut Grove or the Latin Quarter early in the evening, and had come to Scollay Square for a Sally Keith show. If they were lucky, the opening act would be a future television star like Joe Ross of *Car 54, Where Are You?* fame, or comedian, author, and movie star Alan King. Larry Storch, who is probably best known for his role as Corporal Agarn on the television show *F Troop*, worked with others who achieved various degrees of stardom when he played the Crawford.

> I did impersonations and told funny stories. I followed a comedian and singer named Frank Fontaine, who later went on to work with Jackie Gleason. He was the darling of Scollay Square and a good friend of mine.
>
> The headliner I worked with at the time was not Sally Keith but a stripper named LaTisha. LaTisha, the Goddess of the Bodice.
>
> On the bill with me was a black guy named Bobby "Tables" Davis, otherwise known as "Iron Jaw" Davis. He would pick up tables in his mouth and swing them around and tap-dance at the same time. The funny thing was, there was this cafeteria across the street, and I went over there with him and he complained that the crust on the pie was too tough.

For local performers looking for a break in show business, the Crawford House provided not only a wonderful training ground, but a place to develop contacts. Trumpeter Leon Merrian recalls his first few nights:

> I went into the Crawford House when I was just a kid. I supported my family when I was about fifteen or sixteen. I went to the Crawford House with Preston San-diford . . . Sandy. They needed a trumpet player. I was very good at playing growl trumpet, and they were gassed with my playing. We did a lot of blues. There was no pit, we were right onstage.
>
> If we got seventeen or eighteen bucks a week, that was big money. There were no agents at our level. It was all word of mouth. They'd say, "Hey, did you hear about that new trumpet player, he's a bitch, can play high, he can growl," and word got around. The Crawford was fairly animated with a lot of table banging and whistling and all that.

Louie Allegro was a piano player who, like Leon, remembers how the Crawford House served as a de facto employment office for musicians:

> Whenever the big boys would blow into town for a date at the Latin Quarter or some of those other places they'd almost always come by the Crawford House after their

date. They'd almost always be looking for someone to fill in for a drummer or sax player who just left the band. We'd hang out in the restaurant and wait for the word to spread about who needed what instrument. That's how a lot of us got our breaks.

Billy Berube of South Boston was a comic who got his start at the Crawford House:

> When I worked the Crawford House I got a hundred minus ten [one hundred dollars minus his agent's ten percent fee]. Right after the war I was a young comic just out of the service. People would ask me how did I become a comic. I'd say, "Well, I make an ass of myself for nothing, I might as well get paid for it."
>
> I'd get to work just before showtime and work three, up to maybe four or five, shows, but ten to fifteen minutes each stand-up. I was really a buffer while the audience changed between strippers. The audiences were not always the best, so if you weren't a good comic you'd get out of the business real fast. I guess you'd say Scollay Square was my training ground.

Comic Timmy Goldberg remembers the Crawford House hecklers:

> Me and a friend talked the owner and general manager of the Mayfair [another Boston nightclub] into hiring Dick Havalin, a comedian, to work with us. So we go down there where he's playing to tell him. When he heard that, he said, "Well, I gotta do the show now." And he starts to do the show with all these props onstage . . . he used to do some wonderful work. Somebody heckles him from the audience, and he says, "I'll never work this place again," and he walked off the stage through the audience and out the door leaving all his props onstage. Then he came and worked with us.

The Crawford House, like so much of Scollay Square, enjoyed a reputation that was naughty enough to intrigue but not nasty enough to keep people away. Still, visits called for discretion . . . when possible.

> Me and a group went to the Crawford House one night. The dancing was wonderful and the music was great. Now, we had gone there not to be seen but to have a good time. As we were leaving my strand of red beads got caught and all the beads fell on the floor. What an embarrassing moment! (Betty G).

For a boy just entering manhood, the Crawford House was something like dad's hidden copy of *Playboy*. Something special was going on . . . one just didn't quite understand what, which made it all the more curious. Harry Shuris was just such a boy:

> During the war I remember walking down the street with my father and going to the subway stop by the Crawford House. As we passed the Crawford House, I

remember seeing somebody standing in the doorway talking to somebody who was inside. And I'd crane my neck to see what was in there and I remember my dad laughing.

Among the Schwartz family's other properties was a lounge called Jack's Lighthouse, near Sudbury Street. It was one of the more recognizable landmarks in Scollay Square because of the replica of a lighthouse that stood over the marquis. Paul Chivanne, a piano player who worked there for many years, tells one of the sadder stories about Scollay Square:

> In the lounge I played an upright piano, which was against the wall. Billy Hagman, who worked at the Beacon Theatre as an organ player, rotated the gig with me. The other musicians used to call him Pops.
>
> I used to have what I called my "Scollay-Square-am-I-ever-getting-out-of-this-place" blues. I dreamt of working a place like the Coconut Grove. Now, when I was working at Jack's Lighthouse, I remember two cute girls from Charlestown who used to come by every Saturday night. Jack's was not that big a place that you wouldn't get to know regulars, especially when they were cute and you were single. One night, one of the girls came in alone and me and some of the other men wanted to know where her friend was.
>
> "Oh, Helen's gone classy on us tonight," her friend said, "she's being taken to the Coconut Grove."
>
> Later that night a porter came in and told us that five hundred people had died that night in a terrible fire at the Coconut Grove. We assumed the number had to be wrong. It wasn't, of course, and Helen Fallon of Charlestown was among the victims that night.

The Crawford House Fire

On March 23, 1948, there was a three-alarm fire at the Crawford House. Nowhere near the magnitude of the Coconut Grove tragedy, this blaze did not take any lives, but did clear the fifty or so residents from their rooms onto the street. Three people had to be rescued from the building as flames destroyed two floors of the hotel.

Living there at the time were several performers, some of whom were just waking up when the fire started at one that afternoon. Sam Pierce and Bert Carr, who had been rehearsing an act in their third-floor room, escaped by tying bed sheets together and climbing down the side of the building. Pierce had already made his descent when the sheet that Carr was using broke in midair. He fell about one story into the arms of a fireman who had just arrived below their window. Harry Kelly, a fight promoter and owner of the Kelly and Hayes Gym on Hanover Street, also escaped injury.

Sally Keith, Queen of the Tassels (Courtesy of Ann Corio, *This Was Burlesque*, 1968).

Sally Keith, who normally stayed at the Crawford House, had moved out a few weeks before the fire after a robbery attempt in her room. Her appearance at the fire that day gave a writer at the *Boston Herald* the chance to pen this headline and story:

Sally Keith Grinds Her Way into Blaze, Bumps Fireman

Whether performing under a spotlight at the midnight show, or wading through water in the burned-out Crawford House in mid-afternoon, Sally Keith, danseuse and "Queen of the Tassel Tossers" has a true sense of the dramatic — $100,000 worth of it.

Just as the Scollay Square fire scene was beginning to pall — the blaze was under control and hose was being rolled up — the platinum blonde, swathed in furs, tapped through the thinning crowd on her spiked heels, brushing past a policeman guarding the hotel entrance, and strode into the foyer.

She was finally stopped in a soot-blackened stairway by an equally sooty fireman who asked her brusquely where she was going.

"I must get up to my suite," she answered, referring to rooms 209 and 210. "I've got $100,000 worth of costumes, furs and jewelry up there."

The staggering sum nearly staggered the fireman into compliance but not quite. Her list of threatened valuables included a white ermine suit, $6,000; a mink suit, no estimate; a sequin wardrobe used in her "heat wave" act, $4,000; a platinum stole, $3,000; and a white fox cape, $6,000.

The entire wardrobe, including her famed tassels, she valued at $50,000 and the jewelry at the same amount. She did not itemize the latter (*Boston Herald*, March 24, 1948).

Sally Keith never moved back to the Crawford House, although she continued to perform there after the nightclub was reopened. From then on her Boston residence was the Hotel Vendome on Commonwealth Avenue in the Back Bay, where she died in 1967, several years after she stopped performing.

The last episode in the Crawford House fire story began on March 24, 1948, but did not earn its punchline for another thirteen years. The *Herald* had reported the day of the fire that:

Clerk and telephone operator Lillian Maretti of Roxbury was credited with saving several lives by staying at the switchboard until the line went dead, warning all the occupants.

"I did nothing," she insisted, "there was no smoke or anything where I was. I just did what would be expected of me" (*Boston Herald*, March 24, 1948).

For her bravery, Lillian got her picture in the paper — an honor surpassing even Sally Keith and her platinum hair and mink stole — above a caption that read, "Fire Heroine." Thirteen years later Lillian Maretti's picture was in the paper again after she and three other employees of the Crawford House were robbed at gunpoint by two men who escaped with $9,600 in cash from the safe. During the July 20, 1961, robbery Lillian's arms and legs were bound with wire, and adhesive tape was placed across her mouth. This time the caption read "Bound and Gagged."

This was not the first time the Crawford House had been robbed or burglarized. It was such a popular target for thieves that the owners installed a special mechanism that would release tear gas if the safe was forced open. But this didn't stop a gang of thieves from breaking into the safe in June 1954. While the tear gas forced them to make a hasty retreat, they did manage to scoop up more than $2,000 before fleeing.

The Crawford House, much like the rest of Scollay Square, was born of opulence and nurtured by Boston's elite. The end came with a wrecking ball ordered by city planners, who saw no further use for a 120-year-old relic. Lest this sound like too much glorifying of the past, here are the words of piano player Chivanne:

> Back then people would ask where I worked, and I'd tell them Jack's Lighthouse or the Crawford House and I'd get a dirty look or they'd say, "Why don't you get a job in a nice part of town?" Now I tell people like you where I worked and they practically get down on their knees in awe of where I was.
>
> The bottom line is that it wasn't as bad as people say it was back then, and it wasn't as good as we say it was now. It was, however, a lot of fun.

Joe & Nemo's

It was night on the beach at Normandy, several days following the Allied invasion of German-occupied France. Guards had been posted around the allied encampment with the warning, Be careful.

A sudden rustling of bushes drew the quick response of a soldier standing guard. "Halt, who goes there?" he asked.

"Private Smith, First infantry," came the reply.

The voice sounded American enough, but the guard had to be sure, so he started to ask the voice in the dark some questions.

"Where are you from?" he asked the intruder.

"Boston."

"What do you know about Boston?"

"Scollay Square."

"What do you know about Scollay Square?"

"Joe & Nemo's."

"Pass."

And so the world was made a little safer for democracy thanks to a hot dog stand.

Not far from where it first stood is the current home of Joe & Nemo's. Ed Insogna, his brother-in-law Frank Merlino, and Frank's son, Anthony, still operate the business that has been in their family since Frank's father opened the first Joe & Nemo's in 1909. From here on Bowdoin Street, just under the dome of the state capitol, they sell Boston's most famous hot dogs. More than a few sales are accompanied by memories.

There are judges, now working in and around Government Center at Scollay

Square, who went to Suffolk University Law School on Beacon Hill. They recall how they survived on Joe & Nemo's food during their belt-tightening school days. The beef stew, according to one former student, "was fifteen cents and you could stand a spoon straight up, it was so thick with meat and potatoes and vegetables."

West Enders, who were ushered out of their neighborhood some thirty years ago in the name of urban renewal, return looking for remains of the places where they grew up, only to find high-rise apartments or government buildings. And Joe & Nemo's.

> At Joe & Nemo's we used to get hot dogs for a nickel. If my father was out looking for me, he knew where to find me—at Joe & Nemo's. He'd come in and I'd be there sitting by the window eating hot dogs (West End Boston Public Library Collection).

There was the elderly man who, after years away from Boston, came back to find Scollay Square gone, but his favorite restaurant still serving the hot dogs he remembered so fondly. Insogna appreciated the man's compliments and gave him some photos he had of the Square and "a couple of dogs on the house." A week later a hundred-dollar savings bond arrived with a note that said, "Thanks for showing me that some of the good things in life still exist."

It would be difficult to find someone who grew up in Boston who did not, at some point in their life, eat a Joe & Nemo's hot dog. Just as difficult would be finding someone who does not remember Joe Merlino as a warm and generous man. And his family is proud, not only of the financial success of Joe & Nemo's but of the reputation Joe Merlino established for himself and his restaurant. Joe had achieved an American dream. An immigrant (he came from Italy at the age of fourteen), he had succeeded in establishing his own business. But this wasn't just *any* business . . . it was something special, as evidenced by this 1963 story in the *Boston Herald*:

> A real American treat was in store yesterday for a visiting African bishop after giving the invocation at the Boston City Council.
>
> The Most Rev. Caesar Gatimus, auxiliary bishop of Kenya, Africa, told the council, "I have been in this country a little over 48 hours and so have a lot to learn. In a few moments I am going to visit a great American institution."
>
> "Fr. Sullivan is taking me to Joe & Nemo's for a hot dog" (*Boston Herald*, February 26, 1963).

Despite the success that comes with being an institution, Joe was always ready to extend a helping hand, as Ed explains:

> Judge Connely of the juvenile court was a friend of Joe's, and several times asked him to put a youngster who was having a particularly rough time to work. Sometimes that made a difference whether the kid stayed out of trouble . . . just having a responsibility and a paycheck turned them around.

Joe's son, Frank, also remembers:

> One day he gave a job to a down-and-out-of-luck type. They needed a dishwasher so that's what the guy did, he washed dishes. One day he's washing dishes and this reporter who was in for a dog sees the dishwasher and says "I know this guy — he was a professor at Harvard!"
>
> Well, the guy left and straightened out his life because he came back some time later to say that without that job he never would have made it through those rough times.

Of course, most customers remember only the nickel hot dogs and dime pitchers of draft beer, or the incredibly diverse group of people who ate there. Burlesque queens and bums, judges and parolees, cops and robbers, the wealthy and the destitute . . . the whole range of people a city has to offer came to one place. This is the story of Joe & Nemo's.

How Joe & Nemo's Began

Joe Merlino was a barber working in a shop on Howard Street. Outside the shop, Izador "Izzy" Schenker sold hot dogs from a cart. The two men had gotten to know each other, so when Joe bought the Dowd Brothers bar (next to the barbershop), he invited Izzy to move his hot dog stand indoors. This arrangement worked until Izzy grew tired of the bar and left.

Anthony Caloggero, who had worked alongside Joe at the barbershop, took Izzy's place. Anthony was known by his nickname, Nemo. When he was younger, a comic strip called "Little Nemo" featured a boy who was constantly getting into trouble. His parents gave Anthony the nickname Nemo because he reminded them of this character. When Nemo joined the business the two men decided to name their bar and hot dog stand after themselves.

Joe and Nemo were not related when they started the business in 1909, though it was staffed by members of both of their families, like Nemo's brother, Samuel. In 1919, Nemo married a girl named Susan Loverde in a ceremony in which Joe was the best man and Susan's sister, Lillian, was the maid of honor. A year later, another wedding made Joe & Nemo's a one-family business when Joe married Lillian, making Joe and Nemo brothers-in-law.

When Prohibition came, the bar closed. To make up for lost business the family opened a restaurant on Stoddard Street, which ran from the front entrance of the Old Howard to Cambridge Street. The restaurant may have been the smallest in Boston, so small that the two men actually had to sell their hot dogs outside the store, even in winter. Many West Enders still recall Anthony "Doc" Lopez, the man who served them hot dogs from a steaming cauldron on Stoddard Street. In 1928 the city of Boston widened Cambridge Street, cutting Stoddard Street in half and making it one of the shortest streets in the city. Joe & Nemo's, once located in the middle of Stoddard Street, was now at the corner of Stoddard and Cambridge. Since Cambridge Street was one of Boston's major thoroughfares, the restaurant's popularity increased even further.

When Prohibition was repealed in 1933, Joe and Nemo applied for and got one of the first liquor licenses issued in the city. A few years before, Joe had bought the building next to the original location on Stoddard Street. Now that Prohibition was over the brothers-in-law broke through the wall to make a bar and dining area on the second floor. Ed Insogna:

> The hot dog stand was always downstairs. The kitchen was behind the bar, raised about six feet up, so that the waiter had to yell his order to the people up top. Joe or Nemo would ring up the order, and the cook would hand it down.

Prices were low everywhere because of the Depression, but here you found food that was not only cheap, but good, too. A steak dinner was only thirty-five cents. So was a full breakfast consisting of eggs, bacon, home fries, toast, and coffee. But the main reason for going was still the hot dogs. What was it about those things that made them taste so good?

First of all, the dogs themselves were made from a special formula by the New England Provision Company (NEPCO). Secondly was the preparation. Ed Insogna explains:

> We steamed the rolls and cooked the dogs in water. We did not boil the dogs. Never! The skin breaks and that releases the flavor into the water and the dogs don't taste as good. That was part of the secret. People could buy the dogs [uncooked, to take home] and they would come back and say "they don't taste the same." That was probably why.

Some West Enders remember the cauldron in which the hot dogs were cooked:

> They had this one guy behind the counter who used his bare hands to grab the dog and place it on the bun. You couldn't be sure by looking at the guy if he had washed his hands before coming to work, but you figured if he had his hands in that water they must have been sterile.

Thanks to the inexpensive food and great location, Joe & Nemo's soon became one of the most popular places to eat in Boston. Joe and Nemo, both interviewed in 1953 by the *Boston Herald*'s "Roving Eye," Rudolph Elie, indicated just how popular the place was. First, Joe:

> We got three shifts going with 78 men and nine cooks on the jump. We close only for an hour and a half a day, too, shutting down at 3:30 in the morning and opening up again at five and that's only to clean up.

Nemo:

> I guess we're an institution. People come from all over. They heard about us from some sailor or somebody somewhere, and they gotta have "one all around" (*Boston Herald*, November 20, 1953).

What does "one all around" mean, anyway? Joe's son, Frank, has been asked that question many times. He explained the expression to the *Boston Post* one day:

> When my dad first opened up he used to serve hot dogs with mustard, relish, onions and horse radish. But it takes a long time for a customer to order a hot dog with mustard, relish, onions and horse radish. So they just made that up to save time.

The horseradish was eventually dropped from the all-around because, as Frank explained, "the younger generation doesn't care for it." The article continued:

Joe & Nemo's in 1961 (Trustees of the Boston Public Library).

But Frank admits he lives in fear of the day when some really old Bostonian will wander down from the Odd Volumes Club, order one all around, bite into it and then bellow: "What, no horse radish?" (*Boston Post*, February 7, 1944).

Joe & Nemo's advertised in only one place: the program of the Old Howard. Even that was probably unnecessary, since another one of the reasons for Joe & Nemo's popularity was its proximity to the theater. For many theater lovers, a stop for a hot dog before or after a show was considered de rigueur. (The Howard–Joe & Nemo's connection was so strong that when the Old Howard was permanently shut down by the city in 1953, revenues at Joe & Nemo's dropped by over five hundred dollars a day.) This loyalty was good for Joe & Nemo's business, but bad luck for one man:

> I used to go to the Old Howard a lot, which was fine with my wife since she didn't know about it. I'd always stop at Joe & Nemo's before a show for a hot dog "all around." Well, I get home one night and my wife takes one look at me and starts yelling, "You went to the Howard!"
>
> So I figure, how can she know? I just keep denying it, but this just gets her angrier. I said, "What makes you so sure I went there?"
>
> "You've got mustard on your tie. You were at Joe & Nemo's, which means you were at the Howard."
>
> That's when I knew she had me.

Not only did audiences from the Howard go to Joe and Nemo's, but many of the performers made it a regular stopping place, too. Ann Corio, Hindu Wassau, Rose La Rose, and others made Joe & Nemo's a part of the backstage life of the Old Howard. Frank remembers how he met Georgia Sothern one evening:

> I remember when I was a kid (I couldn't have been any more than fifteen), I used to work [at Joe & Nemo's] on Saturdays. Those days they used to have four shows at the Howard. The performers couldn't get out to eat, so at dinnertime we used to send a guy to go and get an order for each individual. I go with him one time, and he says, "Take that tray over to that room over there." So I knock on the door. "Come in," the voice says, so I walk in. Georgia Sothern was there. She was standing there, not a stitch of clothing on her. I'm fifteen years old and I just stopped.
>
> So she says to me, "What's the matter, haven't you ever seen a naked woman before?"
>
> I said "No!"
>
> "Well, now you have . . . you broke your cherry, now put the tray down!"
>
> I went away in the service a few years later and came back, and I'm tending bar back at the restaurant. Georgia was playing the Howard again, and she came in and sat down at the bar. She sits down and looks at me and asks, "Aren't you the skinny kid that brought me my dinner one time, and I didn't have any clothes on?"
>
> "Yeah," I said.

She asked, "Well, have you seen any more naked women since then?"
I said a couple, and she said, "Good, glad to hear it!"

Nemo's brother Sammy became friendly with some of the comedians who worked the Old Howard. Billy (Cheese and Crackers) Hagan was one of his best friends. That's why Sammy was able to get away with some of the practical jokes he pulled on Billy. Like the time Sammy put several slices of toast with mustard into Billy's coat pockets. Billy came back the next day and told him, "I got home and put my hand in my pocket and come up with this gooey piece of toast. My wife wants to know where I got it. I told her, "I don't know." She says to me, 'You son-of-a-bitch, you've been drinking again!' Thanks a lot."

Servicemen swarmed to Joe & Nemo's. When liberty time brought them into Boston, the one thing they did not want to do was spend a lot of time or money on dinner. Lonely months at sea had given them other priorities, so Joe & Nemo's was the perfect place to go. Servicemen of all branches carried a loyalty to the restaurant with them all over the world. Strangers who meet on a battlefield usually begin a conversation by exchanging hometowns. Those from Boston often met the reply of, "Boston! Boy, could I go for a Joe & Nemo's hot dog right now!"

Legend has it that Joe & Nemo's was the site of several reunions for soldiers and sailors who met in the heat of battle during World War II. As shells burst overhead, pledges were made to meet at Joe & Nemo's on such and such a date after the war was over. The prize for loyalty goes to the members of Battery C of the First Battalion of the 211th Coast artillery in Pearl Harbor. Outside their thatched recreation hut at Pearl Harbor, they eased their homesickness with a reminder of happier times: a sign over the door which said JOE & NEMO'S.

Meanwhile, back home the war created a meat shortage which threatened Joe & Nemo's. Rationing was something no American liked but most tolerated for the war effort. The limits of patriotism were stretched, however, when in 1943 the meat shortage left Joe & Nemo's without any hot dogs for several days.

Eating at Joe & Nemo's was an experience. Next to one customer reading a Mickey Spillane paperback was likely to be another thumbing through *The Odyssey* . . . in Greek. An article written during the war described the restaurant:

> The noises are wonderful. Every time somebody yells "one all around" half a dozen voices pick it up. And if a waiter slams a tray hard, or outside on the street one car bangs another, it is considered protocol for all hands to yell:
> "Hit him again. He's got no friends" (*Boston Herald*, February 7, 1944).

A trip to Joe & Nemo's might have even landed patrons in the middle of a wedding. When Vincent Provenzano of South Boston married Virginia Zichello in 1951, Vincent's older brother had a big surprise for the wedding party. "He was going to take us all to the Fox and Hound Club, but instead he took us to Joe & Nemo's as a joke," Vincent recalls. "The whole wedding party was there in their tuxedos, and some guy from the *Globe* took our picture."

In 1955, partly in response to slackening business in a Howard-less Scollay Square, Joe & Nemo's began to open new restaurants in other locations. By the early sixties there were twenty-seven restaurants serving over a million hot dogs a year throughout the greater Boston area and in Florida as well.

Because the scheduled razing of Scollay Square was to include all of Stoddard Street, in 1961 the city informed Joe that his building would be taken by eminent domain. Ed remembers bitterly that "the eighteen thousand dollars for the property barely paid for our moving costs to Summer Street." In June 1963, almost two years to the day after the Old Howard burned down, the last hot dog was sold at Joe & Nemo's in Scollay Square. It was a sentimental day for the regulars, who showed up to pay their last respects to the original home of the Hot Dog Kings.

That night the drinks were on the house for the hundreds who showed up for one last hot dog "all around." Customers sang in the barroom and reminisced as they said good-bye to another Scollay Square landmark. Later that night, after the last teary-eyed customer had departed, Joe Merlino walked around the store shutting off the lights and the appliances, just as he and his family had done in the same store for fifty-four years. Then he walked out onto Stoddard Street, turned, and for the last time, locked the door.

What better symbol than a hot dog stand for such a uniquely American place as Scollay Square? And what better symbol of the American dream than a man like Joe Merlino? It was fitting that he should have closed Joe & Nemo's restaurant on Stoddard Street for the last time and, in effect, officially closed old Scollay Square.

8

Memories of
Old Scollay Square

There are other stories that have not yet been told, stories of less famous parts of the place that collectively was called Scollay Square. Perhaps, then, this chapter is like the box of photographs that somehow never made it into the family scrapbook. These are more personal memories, individual snapshots of smaller, less renowned landmarks that mean as much to some people as the Old Howard or Sally Keith did to the rest of Boston.

The Children of Scollay Square

Scollay Square was the domain of the adult, the place from which all good children were told to stay away. Children like Ruthie, who years later raised her own daughter not far from the Square:

> I lived in the North End, and my mother used to say to me [shaking her finger], "You are never to go down there!" And when mother spoke, mother spoke. I was always afraid to hook school—if my mother or father ever heard about it, I wouldn't be able to sit down for a month! When I was growing up I went to Notre Dame Academy, and the nuns would tell us where we could go and where we couldn't go, and Scollay Square was one of the latter places.

You don't have to be a child psychologist to know what happens when you tell a youngster where he cannot go. So while it might seem unusual, perhaps the best place to start this collection of reminiscences about the Square is with childhood memories . . . like those of Charlie, who was asked why he smiled so broadly when he heard the words Scollay Square:

> I'm thinking about the old days because when we were high school kids we never had any contact with sex and this was a new world. For kids who go through school every day and live a normal life to get into a rough, tough area was exciting. It was an adventure. You can imagine what kind of people were there . . .

Aside from kids who played hooky, there were also those who literally grew up in Scollay Square — not because they were delinquents, but because their families owned businesses there. For them, the Square was a place to explore. Joe Sheriff, who later became a Scollay Square performer, remembers:

> My dad owned Sheriff Press on Hanover Street, just above Kelly and Hayes Gym across from where the Casino would be. I worked at my dad's shop in the twenties, and I remember a lot of activity but very little crime. I remember all the photo places and the eateries . . . not fancy eateries, mind you, but good, wholesome food. A lot of sailors came into the area to the tattoo shops, but my dad never worried about my safety.

Jim's job in Scollay Square didn't last very long:

> At age thirteen or fourteen I worked in Scollay Square as a runner for a company that sent out girls to bars and dance halls to take pictures. After she took the picture I would take the film back to the lab to be developed and then run it back to where it had been taken. That job ended when my father overheard me telling a friend that some of the girls at the lab quite often went topless.

Harry Shuris still has vivid memories:

> My dad and uncle had a place down at 31 Scollay Square. It was called Niagara Shower Baths. It was downstairs. Down there they had a barbershop, shoeshine stand, a tailor shop, and individual shower booths. In those days there were a lot of transients and people who didn't have running water available. So someone could get a suit pressed, shoes shined, and a shower.
> My first recollection is sitting in the barber chair — and I must have been a tyke because I was sitting on the board they used to throw across the arms of the chair.
> When I was ten I used to go in on Saturdays and help out shining shoes or replacing towels after someone took a shower, and cleaning up. Being a youngster, I tended to wander. Now upstairs on the sidewalk, almost directly opposite the entrance was an old fellow named John, who must have been . . . well, when you're ten or eleven everyone over twenty-five seems ancient . . . but he was long in years. He had a magazine stand. He wore forty layers of clothing and jackets no matter how warm

or what time of year it was. And I used to go up there, and he'd say "Hey, kiddo, watch the stand for me," and he'd go down to my dad's place to use the john and I'd watch the stand for him. Then he'd come back and say, "All right pick out a couple of magazines." So I'd pick out a few and read them and return them when I was done. I got into the habit of reading a lot that way.

Next door was John's Coffee Shop. There was a tall Greek with a mustache. I used to go in there for a glass of milk. Across the street there was a photographer: Avery Studios. A guy named Williams owned the studio. I used to go watch him work out in the back room, and I think that is the first place I ever saw a picture of a bare-breasted girl.

Joe Silver was the doorman at the Rialto and he knew my dad. Every once in a while my dad would send me across the street for an hour or two to watch a movie in the afternoon if he saw I was getting bored.

The Williams who owned the photography studio was another infamous character in the Square. Known by the nickname Boody, he not only ran the studio but was a well-known bookie and loan shark. It was characters like Boody who helped give Scollay Square a certain flavor, an undercurrent of the illicit, which enticed and tantalized both children and adults.

Yet the Square also had a virtuous side. Rosalie Warren was the oldest of five children growing up in the West End before World War I, and she remembers one of the things that drew her to the area as a young girl:

As a child I was crazy about music. Now, there used to be this mission on Staniford Street where they had the Salvation Army band. At five every afternoon they would march up to Pemberton Square and play—a drum, a bugle or two, and a couple of ladies wearing bonnets carrying tambourines. And I loved the music so much—me and my brothers would go home singing the songs. Soon we had the whole family singing "Jesus Saves," which wouldn't be unusual except we were Jewish.

Rosalie was there when one of America's greatest composers came to peddle his first big hit:

In the basement of the Woolworth's in Scollay Square, they used to sell sheet music—back then it was a nickel. Well, they had songwriters playing their songs on a piano, trying to get people to buy the music. I remember one day there was a short fellow with square shoulders and big eyes, who all the songwriters seemed to be deferring to. Then he sat down at the piano and played his composition, "Alexander's Ragtime Band." That little man was Irving Berlin!

Sal Tecce, who now owns a restaurant in the North End, where he grew up, remembered that aside from playing in the Square at places like the shooting gallery (which replaced Woolworth's during the war), he also worked in the bowling alley, which was located next door to the Rialto. "I used to set up the pins . . . we

Under new management in the 1920s, the Star Theatre was renamed the Rialto. Because of the clientele at the now open-all-night theater, most people called it the "Scratch House" (Photo courtesy of Rico and Merceline Alvitti).

didn't have automatic anything back then. You took your life in your hands because the customers used to aim for you!"

It was during the thirties that the Rialto Theatre (known as the Star until it was renamed during the twenties), got its nickname: The Scratch House. Open all night, at only a dime for admission, it became a de facto boardinghouse for some of Boston's homeless. If you were brave enough to go inside for a show and unlucky enough to sit in the wrong seat, you soon found yourself scratching your way through the matinee. A regular spraying of the theater didn't seem to do much to rid the seats of vermin, although the perfume smell of the spray did manage to cover up the smell of some of the people who slept there.

The Rialto, however fragrant, did serve a purpose, according to Marty:

In high school, me and some friends used to work at the post office annex around Christmastime. We'd show up for work and then around lunchtime sneak out and head for the Rialto Theatre, which was a hangout for postal workers who paid a dime to spend the afternoon away from all that heavy lifting.

The Casino Theatre

The Casino was located on Hanover Street, across the street from Kelly and Hayes Gym. Originally it served the Italian population (which, by the 1920s, had replaced the Irish and Jewish population in the North End) with movies, plays, talent shows, and operas, all in Italian. North End residents embraced this theater and considered it a vital part of their neighborhood, much in the same way the West Enders had included the Star and Olympia in theirs. But not everyone who went there was from the North End. Carl DeSuze was there too:

I once went to an Italian opera at the Casino. The Italians in the North End were then very lustily ethnic and knew their opera very well. There was a traveling opera company, and they were damn good. But if anybody made a mistake the people in the balcony practically pelted them with oranges. It was an exciting thing to be in an audience that smelled heavily of a perfume that you would smell in Naples or a city in Italy.

Another patron remembers a certain night in 1942:

I saw a famous opera at the Casino. They have this march during the opera, and I've seen that put on at the Coliseum in Rome, and they had hundreds of people. Here at the Casino they had four people! But it was beautifully done with beautiful music.

We came out that night (it was winter during the war and the city had been blacked out since Pearl Harbor), and all of a sudden there were lights on. "What's going on?" we asked. "There's a terrible fire uptown." And so we went to see what happened and were there at the Coconut Grove fire.

The Casino continued its tradition of presenting Italian fare for many years, though opera shared the stage with burlesque when the theater was bought by the owners of the Howard in the thirties. Ralph Saya, a projectionist and spotlight operator for many years at the Casino, recalls a typical day:

I would get in about a quarter to nine for a nine o'clock show, turn on the amplifiers and load the first reel of the first show. Then at nine I'd start the double feature, one A show and one B show. They weren't first run, by the way, since the real money was made from the stage show. The film just bought some time while the people filed in.

At noon the candy butchers would come out. That would take about half an hour. Everything sold was supposed to be lurid and mysterious and, most importantly, from France. One of them actually sold empty boxes. He even told the crowd they were empty. "There could be a watch or a diamond ring, but I'm telling you they are empty."

Then the stage show would begin. There was a four-piece orchestra consisting of a drum, a piano, a trumpet, and a saxophone. One day Helen Green, a stripper, got drunk but insisted on going on because if she didn't she wouldn't get paid. She started out slow and was doing fine until she started going faster and twirled around and fell into the pit on top of the drummer.

The strippers had some tricks. I had a dark blue light on them so it was hard to see, and they'd strip until they would jump backstage at the last moment. Some wore a G-string, which they would cover with black wool so a quick look got the audience thinking they got a flash.

High school kids used to get in by showing up early in the day when the movie was on, and the ticket taker didn't care at that hour. The kids had to look fairly mature to get in anyway. Rather than argue they'd let them in. Also, the theater sometimes got stuffy and they would open the fire escape doors, which were not guarded.

The Casino, much like the Howard, was a haven for those who found the three R's too restrictive:

I went to Cathedral High and thought the Casino was great. Mom had packed a lunch for school, and me and my pals went into the Casino when it opened at nine, which is when school was supposed to start. We'd sit through two movies, which ended at noon. Then we'd eat our lunch while the stage was set up and then we'd watch the stage show for the rest of the afternoon. The show ended about a quarter to three when school was getting out, and me and my pals would get on the subway and go home. The Casino was perfect (Jack R.).

Law and Order in Scollay Square

Scollay Square had a reputation for being wild and bawdy. But the consensus of those who were there is that the Square was not what we would today call dangerous. Trouble, most people agreed, did not find you; you had to look for it. The general assessment of Scollay Square is this: you got what you went looking for. Those who came just to look could do just that without having to worry. Those who came for a taste of the wild life also came to the right place.

What part did the police play in this sense of order? Perhaps the passage of time has made cops seem more effective and people more respectful of authority. Certainly the presence of the military police helped. Additionally, Boston police officers had permanent beats, allowing them to become familiar with people and their habits. (This kind of familiarity is slowly making a comeback in many cities with the return of the beat cop, but back then it was standard police procedure.) Many children of the West End who walked through Scollay Square remember, despite its reputation, the feeling of complete security, thanks in part to the presence of a friend, the beat cop:

> The cop in the middle of the Square . . . I can picture him like I saw him yesterday. His name was Danny. I'd get off the subway and he'd be the first person I'd see. "Goin' to work?" "Yep." And then he'd stop traffic so this little kid could cross the street (Harry Shuris).

> There was a policeman in Scollay Square whose name was Barney McGinnis. No one could have missed this fellow. He stood five feet tall, five feet wide, five feet square. He was the most solid policeman you ever saw in your life. In those days the barrooms were open, and this policeman took care of the whole center. There was nothing that happened that he didn't take care of.
>
> What would usually happen is, in the morning a fellow would get inebriated and act up and Barney would get 'im—he had a way of holding them by the collar. There was a police box by the Crawford House Hotel, and he'd bring them to the box like that and he'd ring the bell, and this wooden paddy wagon would roll up.
>
> In the meantime the drunk would be acting up, kicking and swearing at him, and he'd just hold him out. Now everyone in the Square knew this scene was going to happen. The paddy wagon would back up to the box with Barney holding the guy kicking and screaming at him, and when they opened up the two doors he picked the guy up by the collar and by his belt and he'd swing him up and down four or five times, and in one shot the guy would fly into the wagon and his head would hit the boards at the other end, and it would be quiet.
>
> And that was the end of the drunk. At least until the next day (Barney Shore).

> I remember on snowy days, when the snow was up to my waist, having the cop in Bowdoin Square lift me up and, while he stopped traffic with one hand, carry me across the street so I could go to school (Mike).

Drunken Cats, Whoopee Cushions, and Other Memories

Along the smaller streets and squares and alleyways of Scollay Square were hundreds of businesses of every kind which helped add to the area's flavor. During the thirties, times were hard, and former Boston city councilor Fred Langone remembers the pawn shops in Scollay Square, one of which had been in business for years:

> The Simpson and Loan building was at the corner of Cornhill. All the wealthy people who lost their money during the Depression, whenever they needed money, would go to the Loan company and hock a piece of nice jewelry. Simpson's became known as one of the fanciest pawnshops in Boston, with all the Brahmin fine jewelry. Even the racketeers who were going through hard times would go to Simpson's for some money.

Continuing the tradition started by J. J. Hawes in the 1840s, Scollay Square was home to dozens of photography studios, such as Hochburg's, Falk's, Alvitti's, and the Atlas Photo Studio ("Passport Photos While You Wait"). These studios caused problems for some citizens during World War II, when Scollay Square catered to thousands of sailors on shore leave. Most young girls of Boston were advised to "stay away from those sailors in that place." Many did not heed the warning and spent time in the arms of a lonely sailor. "Some of us considered it our patriotic duty," one woman said.

It was not uncommon for a sailor, hoping to secure a memento of his date in Boston, to convince a girl to have her picture taken with him at one of the photography studios. The finished photo would be placed in the store window so the customer would know it was ready. And so it was that every once in a while the mother of one of those girls, confident that her daughter had obeyed the warning about Scollay Square, would be confronted with a photograph of her daughter and some sailor in the window of a photography shop. "There was hell to pay, let me tell you," said one of those who was caught.

Bars were, of course, abundant in the Square. One could quench a thirst at Marty's, the Tasty, or the Half Dollar Bar. The Half Dollar was famous for the coins embedded in the clear plastic counter top. Pity the poor drunk who, after the bartender had thrown down his change, attempted to pick up the encased coins. Regulars of the Red Hat, a bar near the Old Howard, swear that there was a cat there who drank nothing but beer. Some of them also recall the night of a fire in the bar, when some of the patrons tried to help put it out by throwing beer on the flames. The Old Brattle Tavern, located next to the alley that ran from Cornhill to Brattle Street, was another one of the landmarks that has been all but forgotten since it (and the rest of Brattle Street) was swept away. Reading George Weston on this pub makes one wish to step inside and order one more cold one:

> The unpretentious barroom, founded in 1766, claimed to be, and probably was, the oldest continuously operating tavern in the nation. The tavern, occupying the easterly corner [of Brattle Square] was a small, low ceiling bistro of little beauty but great appeal to a group of good fellows who met there to enjoy a brief interval between the

rigors of the business day and sometimes exacting duties of domestic life. Most of the clientele were lawyers or officials from the nearby courthouse, and the talk was frequently of legal matters, although politics, current events, and philosophy received their proper attention. There was always worthwhile conversation at the Brattle. Sometimes it seemed more of a salon than a saloon (*Boston Ways: High, By and Folk,* 1957).

There were also plenty of restaurants and cafés, like the Crescent Grill, the Hub Barbecue, or Albiani's Lunch, all popular, if not for the quality of their food then for their low prices. Bob Dough, whose father William owned the Sears Crescent building when the city took it by eminent domain in the 1960s, recalled some of the famous people who used to eat at Patten's restaurant, located in the Crescent:

There was a sporting goods store called Iva Johnson's, which was right behind Patten's. I remember that Ted Williams used to go down there and admire the fishing gear in the window before coming up for a sandwich and a drink.

Mayor Curley had the same seat and the same waitress every day. He always tipped her with his traditional silver dollar.

Harry Kelly, the fight manager, used to bring his fighters in for a meal before their bouts. I remember he used to order a steak, which he wanted practically raw, with macaroni and some toast. Then he'd bring them over to the Parker House for a nap before the fight.

Before the Braves moved out of Boston we used to get the National League umpires coming in after a game. They didn't have night games back then so they'd come in about six o'clock with baseballs and give them to the busboys and the bartenders. I still remember Marie Jameson was always their waitress—and she was seventy at the time. They loved her like a mother.

Scollay Square's economy was so diverse that just about every kind of business seemed to have prospered here at one time or another. There was Tanya's Tattoo Parlor, Kelly the Hatter, Sal's Barber Shop, and, to make sure all of your visits to the dentist would be as painless as Dr. Morton intended, the New York Dental Rooms. The original Radio Shack, which grew into a nationwide electronics, computer, and video chain, started on Brattle Street and remained there until 1962, when demolition of the Square began. Epstein's Drug Store, located just below Pemberton Square, was said by many to serve the best egg creams (an ice cream parlor confection that is hard to find these days) in all of Boston.

Thousands shopped at clothing stores like Bond's, Leopold and Morse, or department stores like Houghton Dunton. Nearby was the Six Little Tailors, at the corner of Court and Washington streets. At one time Scollay Square was the wholesale toy and jewelry center of Boston. Young's Novelty Shop sold mostly toys. Still open for business in another part of town is the House of Hurwitz, which sold everything from luggage to appliances. Huberman's, Elm Novelty, and

The signs and marquees which stretch down Howard Street (on the left) and Cambridge Street (on the right) entice us to take a stroll and explore the many stores and shops which occupied the Square during the late 1930s and early 1940s (Courtesy of Joe Flashman).

Globe Sales were also located on or near Hanover Street. New England Doll, across the street, sold just about every kind of doll or dollhouse accessory a child or collector could want.

Jack's Joke Shop was America's first novelty and joke store when it opened in 1922. Harold Bengin, whose father opened the original shop on Hanover Street, now operates Jack's at 197 Tremont Street, several blocks away from Scollay Square. He remembers:

> The Square had a lot of character. It had a lot of warmth. Everything that is missing in these new areas now. It had flavor. There were stores there for fifty, a hundred years under the same family management. You didn't see stores going in and out. Little Walker's Riding Apparel was there for years.
>
> A lot of the owners were characters themselves, almost like a Damon Runyon story. Everybody knew everybody else. Across the street was a pharmacy, Doc Sternin and his brother.
>
> We used to have a lot of characters who came into the store. Including Jack Kennedy when he was a congressman. He came in a few times. Yeah, he was a good egg. No, I don't recall what he bought.
>
> We used to have a lot of girls from the Casino and the comedians would also come in. The girls were really nice, not at all like what you would expect from someone who took off her clothes. The comedians would come in once in a while, mostly to replace a prop like a hat that just got too old or maybe got lost. Steve Mills used to come in and he was a nice guy. So did Lou Ascall.

If there was one dominant theme in these interviews, it is this: Scollay Square was more than just the collection of bars and theaters and stores. It is a reminder of a very different time in America, when the most trouble a kid usually got into was sneaking into the Old Howard for a preview of his manhood. It was a time when a father's word was law, and you listened to your old man — or else! Long before we had ever heard of the hydrogen bomb or Lee Harvey Oswald, there was a place naughty enough to gain a worldwide reputation, but safe enough to take your wife or girlfriend.

I was in first grade when they tore down Scollay Square. I never walked its streets or ate a Joe & Nemo's hot dog "all around" or hooked school to see a show at the Old Howard. That's why I always made it a point to ask in interviews, "What do you miss most about Scollay Square?"

The answer most often given? "Life."

> It was such a joy to live in Boston back then. There was always something going on. You could walk at any time — three, four, o'clock in the morning — and not be afraid that anyone would do anything to you. The clockmaker, the Steaming Kettle, they were always there. You could count on them (Marie).

My wife and I saw them swing the ball the day they first began to tear down the building that housed Sheriff Press and Kelly and Hayes Gym. I felt as though a part of my life was passing by me. It was a sad feeling because it was a good life back then. I worked very hard, as did my friends whose dads had businesses in the area. We worked very hard because that's how we were trained (Harry Shuris).

It was sad to see Scollay Square turned into Government Center . . . all those restaurants and placed we used to hang out torn down. But things change, that's how life is. To see all those places gone, it's still a shame. I miss the camaraderie the most. There was a camaraderie among the musicians. You were never out of work if you could play a good show (Leon Merrian).

It was alive. Everything was alive. You walked by and heard all kinds of music playing from everyplace. The music went on all day long (Bob).

There didn't seem to be as much hatred and polarization. There was more acceptance of people for what they were. You were just an individual, and either people liked you or they didn't. There seemed to be truer friendships (Flo Morrison).

It's a different world today, but you probably already know that. We didn't shut our doors at night. Nobody bothered you. A girl could walk down the street in Scollay Square and wouldn't have any problem (Beverly).

If I was kidnapped and taken blindfolded through the city, I would have known when we were in Scollay Square. There was a certain feeling about that place. It was alive (Ralph Saya).

I worked in Boston in the early fifties, then I moved away for twenty years. I moved back and had an office in Three Center Plaza, and to try and go back to my earlier days and locate Scollay Square as I used to know it was very difficult. To try and even imagine the way it looked compared to the way it is now was very difficult.
It's hard to believe it ever really existed . . . you can't believe what a different life it was (Jim).

Sometimes it is the seemingly insignificant thing that sticks out in another person's memory. Barbara Lee, who played the Howard for many years, said this when asked what she missed the most in Scollay Square:

I miss the White Castle hamburgers the most. Remember the little square hamburgers with the mustard? You'd get into town, maybe eight o'clock in the morning on the train, run to the hotel, drop your luggage, and run for a ten-thirty rehearsal. You'd get a half a dozen of those little White Castle hamburgers that were a dime apiece and a cup of coffee. So while you're waiting to rehearse you'd have breakfast.

And here is a nostalgic gem from a man who was asked about his favorite memory of the Square:

In Scollay Square you could play a pinball machine for a nickel. You'd get five balls, and all you'd need was a score of 29,000 to beat the machine. Today it costs fifty cents and you need five hundred thousand to win one game (Walter, from the West End Boston Public Library Collection).

CHAPTER
9

The Demolition
of Scollay Square

At various times during the two decades following World War II, Boston was described as "a sick city" (*Fortune*, June 1964), "dying on the vine" (*U.S. News and World Report*, September 21, 1964), "a hopeless back water, a tumbled down has-been among cities" (*Boston Globe*). There was little room for argument. *Business Week* reported in 1959 that "Moody's Investor's Service reduced its rating of Boston's general obligation bonds from A to Baa—the lowest of any U.S. city with a population of 500,000 or more" (*Business Week*, December 19, 1959). Only one major construction project had taken place downtown since the end of World War II, when the John Hancock Company added a twenty-six-story annex to its Back Bay facility.

The city's tax base—the amount of taxable property—was lower than just about every other city of its size in the United States. Those properties that were taxed were quite often granted abatements—a lowering of a property's assessed value. The administration of James Michael Curley (in his fourth and final term as mayor, from 1946 to 1950) had also been tainted with charges that the abatements for hundreds of buildings had been indiscriminate. *Fortune* magazine reported that "until 1952, the Boston abatement records were kept at City Hall, reportedly in pencil" (*Fortune*, June, 1964).

Those properties not granted abatements were taxed at a rate twice that of New York or Chicago. A vicious cycle was in progress. Businesses were moving out of the city because of the decline of city services and the high taxes. But without the revenue accrued from real estate taxes, Boston was unable to maintain existing public services, let alone try and implement new ones.

Things began to change in 1949, when John B. Hynes defeated James Michael Curley in a close election for mayor. Hynes immediately began attacking Boston's problems from two directions. First, he sought to heal the rift between Yankee "old money" (the bankers) and the Irish politicians. Aiding him was a new ally — the Catholic Church, which took an active role in Boston's rebirth. Second, he tapped into the federal government, which would provide up to ninety percent of the funds needed for urban renewal to any city that qualified, thanks to the Housing Act of 1949.

Sadly, there were some tragic mistakes. The West End was a forty-one-acre neighborhood of almost ten thousand residents in 1950. By 1959 most of the neighborhood was gone, condemned and taken by eminent domain. The residents, promised a place in the high-rise buildings that would replace their homes, ended up scattered across the metropolitan area. The high-priced apartments were affordable only to people from outside the old neighborhood. This project was immediately recognized as an urban planning disaster, yet a similar plan for the South End was carried out about the same time, displacing hundreds more families in the process.

This was also the era of the automobile. Everybody had a car and wanted to use it, as evidenced by the fact that fewer people used the Boston subway system in 1960 than in 1900. But rather than fight this trend, the city planners went along with it by implementing the Central Artery project. By the time this eight-lane elevated highway through the heart of the city was completed in 1959, it was the most expensive in the United States, costing almost thirty million dollars per mile. It also swept away parts of another neighborhood, the North End, leaving many Bostonians angry and suspicious of urban renewal.

There were successes, too. Most city planners agree that the real achievement of the Hynes administration was luring the Prudential Insurance company to Boston's Back Bay. In 1958, on the site of an old railroad yard, construction began on the 150-million-dollar Prudential Center. This project gave Boston a much needed economic and public relations boost, required to attract more businesses to the hub.

The year 1959 was a pivotal one for Boston. Despite projects (such as the West End) that had left a bad impression, Suffolk County Registrar of Probate John Collins ran for mayor on a platform that advocated even more urban renewal for the city. He also made it clear that if elected, it would not be business as usual. "I told the voters that if they had an unemployed brother-in-law they wanted on the city payroll, they shouldn't vote for me," Collins said of his campaign. His opponent was Senate President John Powers, a man whose old-style politics reminded many voters of Curley. Though Powers enjoyed the traditional winner's support from the banking, newspaper, labor, and political community, Collins won. Collins took this as a mandate from the people of support for his belief in urban renewal.

One of Collins's first acts as mayor was to hire a city planner named Edward

Logue to run the Boston Redevelopment Authority (B.R.A.). Logue had been extremely successful in New Haven, Connecticut, impressing Collins so much that he hired him at a salary even higher than his own. Logue had attended Yale Law School, where his coursework included the study of city planning. But he also credits his success to some rather unusual experience:

> I was a bombardier in a B-24. Bombardiers have nothing to do except for fifteen minutes. We'd fly over Europe for four hours, hit some target in Poland, Austria, or Hungary, and turn around and fly back if we were lucky. You would have done your fifteen minutes' worth of work and you've got nothing to do but look out the window. You've got a great view spread out in front of you, so I really learned a lot from that. I can walk into any city in the world and figure out how it fits together pretty quickly.

The B.R.A. had been created by the Hynes administration in August 1957. After approval by the state, the B.R.A. took over all urban renewal activities from the Boston Housing Authority. In 1960, under Collins's direction, the City Planning Board was abolished and its staff absorbed by the B.R.A., giving that organization complete responsibility for planning, development, and implementation of all urban renewal projects.

The B.R.A.'s first priority was to be a carry-over from the Hynes administration: a government center project to be located in the Scollay Square area. This plan was first introduced in August 1956, although the idea was not a new one. In 1930, William Stanley Parker, who was President of the Boston Society of Architects and a member of the City Planning Board, proposed an early version of the Hynes plan for the Square. The Depression and World War II prevented implementation at that time.

The 1956 plan called for all three levels of government (city, state, and federal) to be housed in publicly funded buildings combined with others that would be privately owned and financed. None of the sectors met this plan with great enthusiasm. To begin with, the federal government wanted nothing to do with Scollay Square, at first proposing to build its new office tower on the current site of the John Hancock building. But Scollay Square was advocated by both Collins and Logue for several reasons. One was its central location in the city. The Square was located between Boston's two major railway stations, within walking distance of six subway stops, and a ten-minute subway or cab ride from the airport. The very location that made the Square so important during its heyday was now contributing to its demise.

Next, Scollay Square's tax base had declined. Incredible as it may seem, the assessed valuation of the site in 1957 was almost a third less than what it was during the Depression. The vacancy rate for businesses was about twenty-seven percent — that was almost a million square feet of empty floor space. Scollay Square was described in various publications as "Boston's skid row" (*U.S. News and World Report*, September 21, 1964), an area filled with "flop houses, bordellos and tattoo parlors" (*Time*, November 6, 1964), and a "slum" (*Business Week*, April 13, 1963). This image was not doing the city very much good, and Collins wanted to see it replaced. Getting that to happen was not easy, though.

The federal government's unwillingness to commit to Scollay Square, combined with a general lack of confidence in the city, threatened to kill the Government Center project in the planning stage. Even before taking office as mayor, Collins had to lobby strongly in Washington to convince the federal government to make Scollay Square its new home. This, combined with a similarly successful lobbying effort at the state level, helped ensure that the project would go forward. Once Collins got into office and consolidated the B.R.A.'s power under the guidance of Logue, Scollay Square's future was virtually assured.

For anyone who might have questioned the high cost of such an undertaking, Logue had the best possible comeback: it would cost the city almost nothing in capital outlay. How did he manage that? The answer lay in his ability to read fine print. The original estimated cost of all the urban renewal projects planned in Boston was $180 million. Under the Housing Act of 1949, the federal government would put up two thirds of the cost, leaving Boston's obligation at $60 million. That total was reduced by half because the state matched whatever funds the city appropriated. Concurrently, Section 112 of the Housing Act of 1961 allowed for federal credits to be extended to Boston to compensate for the lost revenue from the land that would now be used by the government. Since the federal government had been convinced by Collins to build in Scollay Square, the city could recoup another one half of the cost. (As an example of Collins and Logue's fiscal brilliance, by 1964 they had managed to secure over $100 million in promises from Washington, with another $33 million pending, while committing only $72,500 of the city's money in cash.)

On July 28, 1961, it was announced that $23 million had been pledged by the federal government for land taking in Scollay Square, to begin around Labor Day. With funds for the project assured, the B.R.A. soon began surveying the businesses in the area to, according to Logue, determine "a taking policy for the area which will make project sites available for development when required" (*Boston Globe*, August 8, 1961). Despite attempts by certain members of the city council to thwart the project (moves Logue today says were "more visible than real"), the city moved ahead with plans to raze Scollay Square.

The trend among developers in Boston and elsewhere these days is to refurbish existing structures rather than tear them down. Current laws encourage developers to take this approach by offering tax breaks and matching funds. This was not the case in 1960. Only one existing building in Scollay Square (the Sears Crescent) was ever seriously considered for anything but kindling. Government Center would be built from scratch.

Taken in the 1920s, this photo shows the road which led to Pemberton Square from Scollay Square. The Suffolk County Savings Bank's main branch is on the left and Epstein's drugstore is on the right (Author's collection).

The approach to Pemberton Square was replaced by Three Center Plaza. The entrance cut through this building was the result of the compromise in 1967 between court officers and city planners for a front entrance to the courthouse (Author's collection).

The Evacuation of Scollay Square

Once the financing fell into place, the project moved very quickly. It was apparent to many who had seen the West End and Central Artery projects that nothing could stop the cranes. How did the men and women who owned businesses and property in Scollay Square react to this news? It may have been just a coincidence, but beginning with the July 28 announcement of land taking, there was a fire in a Scollay Square business every Sunday for a month. Fires continued to plague the area for years, and it was rumored that a few owners decided to get out with the insurance money rather than take their chances with the city. Most owners, of course, managed to work within the system. Some even welcomed the chance to relocate, seizing the opportunity to expand or upgrade. Despite the discouraging economic numbers quoted before, there were still nine hundred businesses that employed more than five thousand people in the fifty-acre site scheduled for demolition. Even the most confident had questions about the future.

For those who needed help, the B.R.A. opened the Boston Relocation Office at 30 Hawkins Street. A staff of seven people attempted to assist businesses with relocation. In November of 1961, Martin Nolan of the *Globe* interviewed William Adams, one of the relocation officers and wrote:

He's confident that the BRA staff can handle any problem, no matter how exotic.

But there's one isolated problem of a Hanover St. business to which Adams and the others respond with a gulp, blush and resigned sigh. The Casino Theatre houses nearly 100 employees with specialized talents.

Will Irma, Peaches, and Cupcake Cassidy be left shimmying out in the cold? The BRA staff declines a quick and easy answer (*Boston Globe*, November 2, 1961).

The owner of the Sears Crescent building in 1961 was William Dough, who was also the proprietor of Marty's tavern on the first floor of the Crescent, and Patten's restaurant, located around the corner on Court Street. With over a thousand seats, Patten's was Boston's biggest restaurant, employing more than 160 people. In 1961, when the city took all of Scollay Square, including the Sears Crescent, by eminent domain, Dough decided to fight for more money than was offered. Dough's son Robert, who runs Patten's at its current 173 Milk Street location, tells what happened:

We were just a figure, a number in Washington, where all the money was coming from. They offered us a certain amount of money in "pro tanto," which meant we had to accept it and put it in the bank. You couldn't touch it.

My father went out and we hired a very well-known lawyer at the time, because my father wouldn't accept the money.

We went to court around the Christmas holiday, and we had all kinds of testimonials and letters as evidence. We figured with all the juries they could assemble they'd never find twelve or fourteen men who'd never been at either Patten's or Marty's.

We would go [to court] before the holiday season, since the lawyer said everybody would be in a good frame of mind. After two days in front of a jury they went and deliberated on what they thought the property was worth. They came back and said we were owed about three times what the city wanted to pay us.

Mr. Logue was pretty upset about it, but there was nothing he could do, of course.

One of the B.R.A.'s biggest concerns was keeping the evicted businesses within the city, which could not afford to lose any more tax-producing sources. Adding to its headache was the fact that some of the areas under consideration for relocated businesses were themselves slated for renewal. Peter Relmer, project director for the B.R.A., spoke about those fears in an interview with the *Boston Globe*:

> The mortality rates for businesses in the path of the Central Artery was pretty high, about twenty percent. We're hoping, of course, that no businesses will have to fold, but the Federal Government was so interested in the relocation of families that it almost neglected the plight of small business. It wasn't until this year that they lifted the ceiling on what we could pay businesses for moving expenses (*Boston Globe*, November 2, 1961).

Relmer was referring to an amendment to the National Housing Act which allowed a business to bill the city for the entire cost of moving, rather than the $3000 limit that had previously been imposed. Yet this largesse was not extended to all Scollay Square merchants, as reported by the *Globe*:

> Several businesses in the Scollay Square area noted as being in arrears too long in rent will be getting the heave-ho soon. The BRA voted to eject them recently.
> One of the commercial tenants, it was learned, is losing his storage space on Norman St. It develops he's too far behind in his $8-a-month rent. So out of the storage space owned by the BRA goes the man's vehicle he uses in his work — his pushcart (*Boston Globe*, June 6, 1962).

Perhaps most ironic was the plight of several hundred families who had moved into the Scollay Square project area after being kicked out of the West End. Now they would have to endure the loss of their homes to urban renewal all over again. The city was even less generous this time, offering only $200 for moving expenses along with a free relocation service. Almost half the families evicted from Scollay Square moved out of Boston, most of them to Medford and Somerville, north of the city.

The Last Days of Scollay Square

Meanwhile, plans for Scollay Square's replacement continued to be formulated. There was a short-lived proposal that a mayor's mansion and governor's mansion be erected within the Government Center project. The suggestion was made by John P. Ryan, a recent appointee by the mayor to the B.R.A. Collins was quick to stop all talk of such an idea, explaining that it ran contrary to the "image of a city practicing economy" (*Boston Globe*, October 5, 1961).

The final plans made by I. M. Pei and Associates of New York (the architectural firm that would later design the John F. Kennedy Library in Dorchester and the glass John Hancock tower in the Back Bay) were made public on October 18, 1961. One week later an urban renewal first took place in Boston when the entire project area, containing just over fifty acres of real estate, was seized by the city. What made this land-taking so unusual was that the plan for Government Center had not yet been approved.

By taking this gamble, Logue and Collins shaved almost two years off the project. They reasoned that once the plans were approved, with the land already cleared, construction could begin immediately. And so, in February 1962, the demolition of Scollay Square began. The wrecking ball moved in with ferocity, tearing down block after block of Scollay Square, as businesses along each street dutifully moved out. Some good-byes were harder than others. Joe Harrington's byline for many years in the *Boston Globe* was "Sidewalk Superintendent." This is part of his column on the end of a personal landmark:

> The crashing of masonry and the crunching of steel disturbs the meditative mood of customers seeking the solace of food and drink, so three more popular spots in the Scollay Square area have quietly folded.
> The Court Street Tavern (Marty's) at the corner of Cornhill missed its first Monday morning opening in 23 years.
> The wreckers chewing up the buildings for the Government Center haven't yet touched the side of Cornhill where the tavern, the adjoining coffee shop and Eichel's Spa were located, but business fell off and the doors were closed.
> Since February 17, 1939, says John Linehan of Dorchester, the manager, the corner tavern has been meeting the needs of many customers from the courthouse, City Hall lawyer's offices and a lot of guys who dropped in to chin with the inn-keeper, the late Marty Clougherty.
> Marty didn't drink but he was blessed with a sympathetic ear for those who did.
> For some years before he opened the place on the corner, Marty operated the Pen and Pencil club in the upper floors of the building, which gave late service to night workers and others who kept late hours (*Boston Globe*, June 19, 1962).

The Pen and Pencil Club was a well-known speakeasy during Prohibition. With repeal, Marty went legitimate and obtained one of the first liquor licenses in the city. He owned and operated Marty's tavern until old age forced him to retire and sell the place to William Dough, the owner of Patten's.

The Government Center project had removed much of Scollay Square by the fall. It wasn't until October 18, 1962, however, that the traditional groundbreaking ceremony was held. Judging from the shape of the Square, which by then resembled one of those bombed-out cities that Ed Logue had viewed from his B-24 during the war, the ceremony seemed a little redundant.

City Hall

Another unique aspect of the Government Center project was the plan for City Hall. The Government Center Commission, which had been established by the state legislature in 1958, recommended that the job of designing the new building be left open to a competition. Similar ideas had produced plans for the widely admired Toronto City Hall and the Dublin Trinity College Library.

Former Mayor Collins recently recalled:

> The competition was the only serious disagreement that Ed Logue and I ever had. Logue said, "There has never been a public building built as a result of a public competition in fifty years of public works and the reasons were good. When a competition is held the client, the city, bastardizes the job by refusing to accept the winner." I said we were going to go ahead with it and we did.

By October 1961, the commission was ready to begin the competition. Maps and brochures of the area were mailed to more than three hundred architects vying for the $5000 first-round prize. As a demonstration of the city's willingness to be fair, none of the judges would know the names of the architects. Eight semifinalists were chosen in the early spring of 1962, at which point they were asked to submit further details of their plans.

On May 3, 1962, the winner of the competition was announced. Three Columbia architecture professors, Gerhard M. Kallman, Noel Michael McKinnell, and Edward F. Knowles won the approval of the Government Center Commission to design Boston's City Hall. Selection by the committee did not mean they had the job, however, just the prize for winning the competition. Now the city and the Federal Urban Renewal Administration had to decide if they would use the plan. While they deliberated, the public got a chance to voice its opinion.

To say that reaction to the design was mixed is an understatement. Judging from articles in architectural magazines, letters to the editor in daily papers, and speeches made before architects and laymen alike, there was no middle ground on the subject. People either hated the design or loved it.

Edward Durell Stone, speaking on May 12, 1962, before 300 engineers and architects at the annual spring meeting of the Society of Military Engineers, said, "It looks like the crate that Faneuil Hall came in."

Horizon magazine, a monthly publication dedicated to the field of architecture, remarked that the design had "a style that ranges from WPA post-office colonial to Neo-Facist Federal" (*Horizon*, January 1963). Other critics, also dissatisfied with the choice, labeled the structure "terribly confused," "a hodgepodge" (*Horizon*, January 1963), a "Cheops Tomb," a "pigeon cage," and a "chinese pagoda" (*N.E. Newsclip*, January 31, 1968). Some critiques were more practically based. Noting the large open area in the middle of the building, one person wanted to know what would happen to all the snow that fell in the atrium.

Taken after the removal of Cornhill and Brattle Street in 1962, this is a rare view of the length of Hanover Street from the American House (barely visible on the far right) to Arrow Sales (on the left end of the block). The John F. Kennedy federal building replaced this block of stores in 1964, and Hanover Street was paved over to make way for City Hall Plaza (From the collection of Irene Shwachman).

Defense of the Kallman, McKinnell, and Knowles design came from people both in and out of the profession. It was, according to some, "highly poetic — an expression for the future" (*Boston Globe*, June 1, 1962), "exciting and different," and "dramatically conceived" (*Boston Herald*, May 27, 1962), "anything but a weak-kneed copy of the state house dome" (*Boston Globe*, June 15, 1962). Critic Ada Louise Huxtable called it a "subtle, dramatic, respectful homage to the past by an uncompromising present" (*Horizon*, January 1963).

In what many saw as a bold statement for a modern Boston, the Government Center Commission approved the design of City Hall on June 28, 1962. This cleared the way for the three architects to begin work on details of the project, which were due in a year. The city would use the time to select the construction companies who would prepare the site and start the foundation work.

Work on the foundation required the realigning of subway tunnels under the plaza, since City Hall was to sit directly over the section of subway which ran from Scollay Square to Adams Square. As it turned out, city planners had a use for some of the old tunnels. Part of the subway was converted into an underground delivery tunnel for trucks and vans. The rest was supposedly filled in. But in 1983 a city worker opened up a door in the basement of City Hall and discovered an un-touched piece of the original 1898 subway tunnel which had connected Scollay

Square with Adams Square. The city, desperate for storage space, contracted a company to clean and waterproof a 150-foot section of the tunnel. Electricity and a dehumidifier were installed, and today the tunnel is used to store old city records.

Soon after the demolition of the Square had begun in 1961, work started on the relocation of the Scollay Square station from the middle of Cambridge Street to the plaza. The new Government Center station opened a year after the ground-breaking for City Hall, on October 28, 1963.

Boston watched its new city hall rise with a mixture of pride and curiosity. In 1967 it was apparent that the building, two years behind schedule and costing $5 million more than originally planned, was not going to be ready for use by Mayor Collins, who had decided against running for another term. As a way of displaying his committment to the new structure, near the end of his administration Collins set up his office in the still unfinished building.

Whether one thinks of it as a monument to a modern Boston or a slap in the face to the old one, City Hall is a remarkable structure. More than 15,000 separate chunks of concrete, many of them precast, had to be set into place during construc-

Taken from the Custom House Tower, this photograph shows Scollay Square during the mid-1950s (Courtesy of the B.R.A.).

The Square during the construction of City Hall in 1966. At the end of One Center Plaza (in the upper left-hand portion of the photograph), the Beacon Construction company had let everybody know that their project was "TO BE CONTINUED" (Courtesy of McKinnell and Wood).

Government Center today. Just behind the new City Hall (in the middle of the photograph) is the John F. Kennedy federal building (Photo by Mauzy).

tion. In some places eight had to be joined together at one point. Early critics of City Hall claimed that it looked like a fortress. That may or may not be true, but considering that it was designed to last 150 years, City Hall will probably outlast those critics.

One Two Three Center Plaza

As construction progressed on City Hall, the wrecking ball was making quick work of what used to be fashionable Tremont Row. What the cranes were removing in 1963 and 1964 were mostly tattoo parlors, passport photo shops, and pawnshops. Replacing these relics of Scollay Square's last days would be the first private office building in Government Center. Designed by Welton Becket and Associates, developed by Norman and Robert Leventhal, and built by the Beacon Construction Company, One Two Three Center Plaza stretches along the base of Beacon Hill from Tremont Street to Bowdoin Square. It was and is widely praised for, as one B.R.A. member stated, its "use of color, texture, and scale. The red brick, the precast concrete and glass—all of these materials give life to the form of the building, and effect a transition between the old and the new Boston" (B.R.A. Design Advisory Committee, September, 1963). The building, if placed on one end and straightened out, would stand more than seventy stories high, prompting Walter Muir Whitehill to call it "a skyscraper mercifully laid on its side" (*Boston: A Topographical History*, 1968).

The project was divided into three phases, one for each building, due mainly to the developer's uncertainty of Government Center's success. With a touch of whimsy, as each of the first two phases were completed, the construction firm marked the end of the buildings with the words: "To be continued." Construction on the first two pieces of the giant complex went smoothly. The third and final part was stalled for months in mid-1967 because of two battles. One was between officers of the court and the B.R.A. over automobile access to the Courthouse in Pemberton Square.

The plans called for blocking off Pemberton Square from all vehicular traffic. Logue and the B.R.A. wanted to build a tree-lined pedestrian walkway between the back of Center Plaza and the front of the old Courthouse. But members of the judiciary decried the idea of a courthouse without automobile access in the front. There were also questions about emergency vehicle and handicapped accessibility. Logue, arguing for the B.R.A. plan, said, "We felt there should be a pedestrian entrance that would be much better, easier and convenient. They [the judges] want a highway kept there. We think it will just become a privileged parking lot" (*Boston Globe*, July 15, 1967). As the two sides debated, some began to wonder if the "To be continued" sign on Two Center Plaza would have to be changed to "The End."

The issue was resolved with a compromise, of sorts. Pemberton Square is closed to vehicular traffic, although emergency vehicles can make their way onto the brick walkway if there is a need. Furthermore, a large entranceway was constructed through Three Center Plaza which includes an escalator. The agreement hammered out between the court and the B.R.A. states that Beacon Construction must keep the escalator running during court hours.

The other roadblock to completion of Three Center Plaza came from owners of property on Tremont Street. J. I. and Abraham Moskow, two local developers, claimed that the B.R.A. did not have a marketable title to the land. These two brothers had already stalled for two years the construction of the New England Merchants National Bank at State and Washington streets with a case that was eventually lost in the Supreme Court. The B.R.A. managed to avoid another lengthy and costly wait by including a clause in the construction company's contract ensuring them that they would not be held responsible if the Moskow brothers won their case. This allowed Beacon Construction to finish the rest of One Two Three Center Plaza without fear of a lawsuit. The brothers eventually abandoned their case.

George Gloss and the Sears Crescent Building

Controversy also dogged the Government Center project from another direction. The plans to raze all of the buildings in Scollay Square drew the attention of local historians, who argued that several of the buildings, most notably the former home of Garrison's *Liberator* (located on Cornhill near Faneuil Hall), should be saved. George Gloss, who at that time owned the Brattle Book Shop in the Sears Crescent Building, joined the fray.

George had been hired by the original Brattle Book Shop in 1948 to help with a going-out-of-business sale. With $500 from his recent wedding, Gloss and his wife bought a half interest in the store and kept it open. Later, in the fifties, when Colesworthy's (another famous Boston bookstore) was going out of business, he bought it and moved it to Cornhill. Gloss had a knack for publicity. Each time demolition forced him to move his bookshop around Scollay Square, he would hold great giveaways. These events became local front page, even national news, as thousands of people lined up for hours to take advantage of George's simple offer: whatever you could carry after five minutes in the shop you could keep — for free. With four giveaways in Scollay Square, Gloss gave away almost a quarter of a million books.

Gloss kept his last bookshop on Cornhill open until the very last possible moment. His son Ken, who owns the Brattle Book Shop, which is now located at 9 West Street in Boston, remembers:

In order to get the customers in the store, customers had to watch the wrecking ball. As it swung back you could get in the building, but when it moved forward you were stuck where you were. It wasn't very good for business.

George Gloss in front of his Brattle Book Shop (Courtesy of Mrs. George Gloss).

Cornhill during one of George Gloss's famous book giveaways (Courtesy of Mrs. George Gloss).

The magnitude of the Government Center project prevented Logue from ex-cluding every historically significant building from demolition (such as Garrison's *Liberator* building, which was torn down to make way for City Hall), but Gloss and a number of historians eventually convinced him to save the Sears Crescent Building. In his report to the B.R.A. in January 1968, Logue wrote:

> From a design standpoint, the height and mass of the building will complement new buildings within the project.
> For example, the curving facade of the Sears Crescent has its counterpart in the curved office building to be built between Scollay and Bowdoin Squares.
> The red brick facade will also enhance the red brick base of the new City Hall, and the paving of the Government Center plaza.

The Sears Crescent, Logue concluded, "is a ready made link between the past and the present" (*Boston Globe*, January 20, 1968).

He was met with opposition from several sources. Robert Morgan, chairman of the mayor's City Hall Commission, was reportedly against the idea, believing the red brick building would detract from the modern Government Center. City Councillor William J. Foley was a longtime foe of saving any of the original build-ings in Scollay Square and said so even before land-taking began:

Cornhill during the 1920s. The site of Garrison's *Liberator* building was at the far end of the street toward Faneuil Hall. Visible along Brattle Street (to the left of Cornhill) are the Quincy House and Leopold Morse and Company, which replaced the Brattle Square Church (Courtesy of the Bostonian Society/Old State House).

I'd rather have visitors to Boston look at things they see in Miami and New York — bright shiny tax producing buildings, rather than some ugly building where William Lloyd Garrison once published the Liberator. . . . It just doesn't make economic sense (*Boston Globe*, July 25, 1961).

The Government Center project had been divided into parcels, each one designated for either city, state, federal, or private use. The Sears Crescent building, along with three other buildings bounded by Cornhill, Court Street, and Franklin Avenue, was partitioned off into parcel number ten, designated for private development. For some members of the city council and the B.R.A., the question was not the historical significance of the Crescent building, but the monetary benefits of parcel ten. In late 1963, the word went out from those who had advocated the removal of the building, that if a developer could be found willing to bear the cost of refurbishment, the Crescent could remain in the plans for Government Center.

In 1967, the Development Corporation of America, based in Boston, won approval from the B.R.A. for its plan to refurbish the Sears Crescent building. I. M. Pei was instructed by the city to include the Sears Crescent in his plans. Ken

The *Liberator* building and all of the bookstores are gone now, but the Sears Crescent Building still marks the graceful curve of what was once Cornhill. Brattle Street was replaced by City Hall plaza and Brattle Square by City Hall. The Government Center at Scollay Square subway station is at the bottom left hand corner of this photograph (Author's collection).

remembers Pei coming into the shop saying, "I wish I had known this was historically significant. It will cost thousands to change the plans now."

Visitors to City Hall Plaza usually agree that the change was worth the extra effort. Three sides of the plaza present the pedestrian with glass, steel, and concrete visions of a bureaucratic future: Boston's City Hall, the federal government's John F. Kennedy building, and the privately owned One Two Three Center Plaza. On the fourth side, thanks in part to George Gloss, we still have the Sears Crescent building — a graceful, red brick reminder of how Boston used to look before people designed cities with pocket calculators.

The Rest of Government Center

Other aspects of the Government Center project included the John F. Kennedy federal building, which was named for the slain president upon completion in 1964. It replaced the block between Hanover and Sudbury streets. (Hanover, which had run all the way into Scollay Square, was paved over between the J.F.K. building and City Hall.)

Taken just after the Scollay Building was torn down in 1871, this is a rare view of an empty Square during its heyday (Courtesy of the Bostonian Society/Old State House).

Scollay Square's demise was imminent when this photograph was taken in 1962 (Courtesy of the B.R.A.).

Government Center at Scollay Square today. A cleaner, more streamlined place, perhaps, but certainly not as much fun (Author's collection).

Boston's first new police station in thirty-five years opened in 1968 on New Chardon Street. Called a "model station" by the police department, it was the first police station built in the city that had air-conditioning, a luxury to which a street cop was not then accustomed. A 1900-car garage, over what used to be Haymarket Square, was under construction in early 1968 when the new mayor, Kevin White, suggested a heliport be placed on top of the nine-story structure. The idea was rejected by the city as too dangerous, and the parking lot was completed without a landing strip. At this writing however, twenty years after completion of the lot, construction is underway on several stories of office space on top of the building.

Technically, the Government Center renewal project is still not finished today. Parcel six, which stretches behind City Hall along New Congress Street, was scheduled to include a motel complex and parking garage. Instead, a small parklike walkway leads pedestrians from the Haymarket subway station to a revitalized Faneuil Hall and Quincy Market. Given the congestion from surrounding projects, it is unlikely that the city will allow development of this land. Along this park, near the back of City Hall, stand two statues, both of former mayor and Boston legend James Michael Curley. One wonders what hizzoner, if suddenly brought back to life, would think of his successors' work. He was, at times, known to partake of Scollay Square's delights. How do you suppose he'd react when told that the stage where he used to watch Ann Corio from his front row seat was now a park bench? Would he be nostalgic? Would he chalk it all up to progress? Would he be angry? Perhaps he'd start a reelection bid for a fifth term with a new slogan: "Bring Back Scollay Square!"

That's just what some people, in various ways, are trying to do . . .

CHAPTER 10

Scollay Square Returns

Scollay Square may have disappeared from the map, but it isn't gone from the hearts and minds of the people who made it a special place. While most are content to let their memories fill the void, others have found creative avenues through which to recall the days of the Old Howard, Joe & Nemo's, Sally Keith, and the Crawford House.

Theater

In 1985 the North End Union presented an original musical written by John Brenner called *Those Were the Days: A Musical Memoir Album of Good Old Scollay Square*. An admitted Scollay Square lover, Brenner revels in the mix of characters there and reviles in the forces of progress that tore it all down. In his show Brenner managed to capture some of the flavor of the Howard Theatre and Scollay Square, including the candy butcher and the city censor. In the program, he wrote about his feelings toward the Square and the times it represented:

It was an area that was colorful with life, particularly during World War II. I don't know of a serviceman who did not know the fascination of the square! It served almost as a magnet for those escaping the terror of the times. The square had color, characters and constant fascination for all those who passed through the streets. It was not by any means attractive but it did have an attraction. It was an area of innocent sophistication. The buildings were old and cramped together, yet each nook and cranny had a mini-history.

The square was an enigma. There was a unique combination of the very old and the very new of the times. It had a strange color of moods: the gray of years and the flashing neons of now! It was a unique conglomeration of people, places and things. The square never knew night or day, life was there twenty-four hours. It was a place of laughter, escapism, tears, joy, happiness and sadness. Its population was a true mix of Cafe Society of the times to the dregs of humanity, and yet there was an ideal blend, a sort of human understanding, that sadly does not exist today. In the square there were no strangers.

Other playwrights saw more in the story of Scollay Square. In 1987 the Nucleo Eclettico Theatre, on Hanover Street in the North End of Boston, presented another original musical about Scollay Square called *Cherry*. It came out at the time the city and state were finalizing plans for the depression of the Central Artery, the six-lane elevated roadway that had effectively cut the North End off from the rest of the city when it was built in the fifties. Construction of an underground artery would greatly affect the people of the North End, and *Cherry* attempted to explore the similarities between the Scollay Square demolition and the current reconstruction of Boston, while at the same time bringing back memories of the sailors' home away from home.

Banned in Boston, a 1988 Theatre in Progress production, used the 1933 closing of the Old Howard as a centerpiece for a look at censorship. Unlike Mr. Brenner, who had lived through the era, playwrights Amy Ansara and James D'Entremont were not even alive when the Howard closed in 1953, making their task difficult. Yet they managed to explore the issue of censorship in Boston while faithfully recreating some of the innocent naughtiness that went on in front of and behind the curtain of the Old Howard.

Books

Scollay Square's reputation has suffered in most books written since the demolition; it is almost never used as an example of Boston's exciting history, but rather as a symbol of the dying inner city.

In *The Making of the President, 1960*, Theodore H. White chronicled the election process with the race between John F. Kennedy and Richard Nixon. The book begins on election day in Boston as candidate Kennedy casts his ballot at the West End Branch of the Boston Public Library on Cambridge Street. From there, a motorcade took him to the airport and a waiting plane. But first, as the narration continues, "it moved swiftly out of the West End, down through the grimy blight of Scollay Square, under the tunnel to East Boston and the airport" (*The Making of the President, 1960*, 1961).

In *Back Bay*, a sweeping historical novel written by William Martin and published in 1979, the Square is again described in less than complimentary terms:

He hurried down Beacon Hill, past the courthouse, and into Scollay Square, where the lunchtime crowd was gathering. Lunch in Scollay Square: two drinks in the Domino Lounge watching Shirl the Twirl and her tassels; the mid-day show at the Old Howard, a burlesque house where your feet stuck to the floor and your pants sometimes stuck to the seat; or a half hour with the lady of your choice in a rundown hotel (*Back Bay*, 1979).

To be fair, the descriptions *were* apropos for the times. As we have seen, the Square declined greatly after World War II as Boston moved into an era of stagnation. Both White and Martin seized upon Scollay Square as an example of Boston's dire economic situation during the fifties and early sixties.

Scollay Square has never, until now, been the sole subject of a nonfiction book. The Bostonian Society did publish a thirty-two-page booklet with the rather heady title of *The Metamorphoses of Scollay and Bowdoin Squares*. Written by the late Walter Muir Whitehill, it consisted mainly of excerpts from his masterpiece, *Boston: A Topographical History*, that pertained to the two squares.

Ann Corio's *This Was Burlesque* gives us a wonderful view of the Old Howard from one of its biggest stars, along with stories about other burlesque stars and the theaters they played in around the country. Ann (who today runs the Encore Dinner Theatre in St. Petersburg, Florida, with her husband) is currently trying to get the book reprinted.

The one book dedicated to the subject of Scollay Square is a novel written by a Radcliffe graduate who grew up on Beacon Hill, not too far from the Square. Pearl Schiff had to wait until she got married before she could sample the hangouts in the Square, since her mother had made it clear that it was one place she was forbidden to visit alone. "I found it fascinating," she told me, "so we started spending Saturday nights there and for two or three years I just kept notes and worked at it."

The novel centers on Beth Prentiss, a young girl who leaves her high-class world of teas and coming-out parties to live on her own near Scollay Square. There she meets Jerry Blake, a seaman who looks upon women and liquor as things to be used for his own pleasure. A streetwise hooker, an innocent farm boy who has just joined the service, a proper lawyer who shuns the Square (but loves Beth), and an assortment of other characters that Pearl "borrowed" from real life also fill the story.

In 1951 Schiff found an agent, who sold the book to Signet Publishing of New York. Schiff proudly reports that, "A year later *Scollay Square* made the national bestseller list. In the year of Hemingway, Wouk, and Steinbeck! I was on the same list as them for a short three weeks. Maybe in another year it might have done better." *Scollay Square* was both a commercial and critical success. Schiff was praised for her attention to detail and ability to weave a true picture of the Square into a novel. The *Boston Post* critic wrote that:

Scollay Square is a remarkable first novel, because it completely succeeds in reaching its planned climax and goal. It is not a book for the young or the overly prim reader, any more than a frank case study would be. And if anyone reads the book only for a leer, he is just as cheap as the average wandering gob who was satisfied with the company of anything at all wearing a skirt (*Boston Post*, August 31, 1952).

What did Schiff's alma mater think of her literary effort? "I never had much feedback. It went into their library. I remember one comment in the *Radcliffe Quarterly* on 'How come Pearl Schiff has such a negative point of view on religion and family life?' That's the only mention at Radcliffe I got!"

If Scollay Square can be said to live at all today, then it is in the pages of, believe it or not, a comic book. *The Jazz Age Chronicles* is a detective story set in Boston during the 1920s. Created by the team of Ted Slampyak, Marc Gacy, and Dan Neff, it is a bimonthly publication which, within an aura of mystery and intrigue, effectively re-creates those times. The lead character, a hard-boiled detective named Ace Mifflin, has his office in the Sears Crescent building.

Ted Slampyak's drawing are not only artistically well done but they are historically accurate. Every detail of Prohibition-era Boston and Scollay Square has been presented, right down to the marquis of the Old Howard, which displays the acts that actually appeared on the day the action in the story is taking place. If you are looking for a way to, as Ted puts it, "feel you're walking through 1926 Boston, smelling the cheap liquor on a sailor's breath in Scollay Square," then look for *The Jazz Age Chronicles*, published by Caliber Press.

Art

When City Hall Plaza was first opened to the public some believed it would have a great effect on Boston. One architect predicted that the plaza would be like St. Peter's Square in Rome, acting like a giant magnet to which people would be drawn. Anybody who knows Boston can tell you that the exact opposite happened. Lonely and barren, the plaza is one of the windiest places in what is already a very windy city. Since there are only government and private offices surrounding it, about the only thing open after five o'clock or on weekends is the subway station. Quincy Market and Faneuil Hall are located just behind City Hall, so any pedestrian traffic tends to head for that part of the waterfront.

City Hall itself is the subject of much discussion of late, as Boston begins to debate its effectiveness for public service. The original intent made a lot of sense: put the most frequently used departments on the lower floors (tax collection, construction permits, and parking fines) and the departments requiring less public access on the upper floors. But the result, according to many citizens, is gray, winding, poorly marked hallways that present an imposing symbol of confusing city bureaucracy.

That is why the May 1988 display of antiestablishment art in one section of the building was such a surprise. If anything represents the establishment it is City Hall. Yet it was here that "The Chapel Project: A Journey into the Future" was presented. Six local artists got together to create a multimedia exhibit that explored the past and present use of the Scollay Square site.

One of the works was a grass map of Scollay Square before demolition, created by landscape artist Linda Cook. Cook found a lot of people curious about her work, "and when I told them it was an abstract map, they would look kind of disappointed and say, 'Oh,' but when I said the map was of Scollay Square their eyes lit up and they suddenly become very interested."

Jerry Beck's sculpture, *In Search of Moby Dick and the Tattoo Palace*, combined his love of the Melville novel with the history that Scollay Square shares with sailors from all over the world. A monumental installation located in the central atrium of City Hall, Beck's work featured huge fishing nets dotted with little sailboats, oars, rope ladders, and antique photos of boats and harbors.

The show ran for a month and was welcomed by critics and city workers, some of whom had never realized that the building in which they worked had a central atrium.

Scollay Square, the Horse

My uncle John advised me one day during the summer of 1989 that had he and I been at Rockingham Racetrack in Salem, New Hampshire, over the previous weekend we "would have lost a fortune."

'Why?" I wanted to know.

"Because a horse named Scollay Square came in second in the fifth race, that's why."

A quick glance at the racing form in the paper confirmed my uncle's story. I was both amused and delighted. I had read books, heard songs, seen plays, art exhibits, and even comic books on Scollay Square, but this was truly the most unique way that anyone had found to remember it.

The horse is owned by Frank Reed, who grew up on the streets of Revere and today is the founder and owner of the highly successful home and automotive loudspeaker manufacturing company, Boston Acoustics. Frank and his wife, Dorothea (a former West End girl who lived on Green Street before getting married), only recently got involved with horse racing but have developed a small passion for the sport. Frank talked about the circumstances surrounding this horse:

> About five years ago I had a chance to buy a filly whose father was named Soldier Boy and whose mother was named City Woman. I grew up in Boston and remember the Square and so it just seemed natural to name her Scollay Square.

Now in her second race, she ran at Suffolk Downs Racetrack on "West End Day." She came in second to a horse named Look Me Up In Boston. Last June she was part of a Daily Double. The winner of the first race was Sipsy Rose Lee [you can't name horses after famous individuals without their consent], and Scollay Square was the winner of the second race! All the old guys at the track won the Daily Double that day because they all bet on Sipsy Rose Lee and Scollay Square!

Frank Reed has a great affection for this particular horse, one of several he owns. He says that "she has come into the money over fifty percent of the time. She's small, but gamey. She's got no class but she's all heart." Just like her namesake.

The Renaming

After more than thirty years on radio, talk-show host Jerry Williams has become the master of taking popular issues and turning them into big ratings for his station. After one term in office Boston Mayor Raymond Flynn was equally adept (as most politicians are) at finding ways of getting good publicity. Put these two men together in an election year and you have a powerful force for change.

On June 20, 1986, the city of Boston held a celebration for the recently crowned champions of basketball, the Boston Celtics. Thousands of people jammed the streets to view a parade honoring the team. The parade ended at City Hall Plaza, where the stars could be lauded by their fans. Down below, among 200,000 screaming people, Jerry Williams was broadcasting his radio program on WRKO.

When the ceremony ended, the crowd quickly dispersed and the plaza soon returned to its normal empty state. This left Williams alone for the remainder of his program. He began the post-Celtics portion of his show by declaring that he was broadcasting from "Scollay Square, not Government Center!" For the next two hours Williams took phone calls from listeners who helped him remember what the Square was like before it was torn down. Then an idea popped into his head. Williams declared that he would launch a campaign to convince the city that City Hall Plaza should be renamed Scollay Square.

The issue was certainly not a controversial one. A quarter of a century had dulled many of the seedier memories of the Square, and people were quick to support something that would help bring back "the good old days," if only in name. Enthusiasm for the idea was immediate and practically unanimous among Williams's listeners and the mayor's office. City bureaucracy being what it is, though, the wheels turned slowly. Radio being what it is, the topic was not rushed, either, since the name change was one of the most popular topics on Williams's show during the year it was being planned. Ann Corio was contacted and lent her name and support to the effort. Old-style politicians like the popular city councillors Albert "Dapper" O'Neil and Fred Langone joined in the campaign, too. (O'Neil, by the

April 29, 1987. His renaming campaign a success, talk show host Jerry Williams watched as Mayor Raymond L. Flynn (left) read the proclamation which officially returned the name Scollay Square to Boston (Author's collection).

way, had been involved in a privately sponsored ceremony in 1977 in which a plaque commemorating Scollay Square was placed at Two Center Plaza by a local businessman.)

Heading the mayor's office on Cultural Affairs was Rosemarie Sansone. She had her own connection to Scollay Square, since her uncle Dixie had owned a number of clubs and bars there, including the Red Hat. Leading the charge for Williams was his trusty producer, Alan Tolz. His job was to arrange publicity for the renaming, a major part of Williams's plan. Finally, the mayor's office selected April 8, 1987, as the day that Scollay Square would officially get its name back. Local and regional newspapers were informed and most seemed to favor the idea in their editorials. The *Boston Globe* wrote:

> Now there is a proposal to bring back the old name. It should be done—as quickly as the street signs can be changed.
>
> There is some irony in the fact that the old Scollay Square was as much a center of government as its replacement is. The coffee shops and bars on the tangle of streets that led toward the State House, the old City Hall and the Suffolk County courthouse were where the politicians of last-hurrah days met to hatch deals and concoct strategy.
>
> It was pure Boston, as was the name (even if none of the Old Howard's customers cared what kind of business the original Mr. Scollay was in). And the song that mentions the Scollay Square station—where Charlie's wife handed him a sandwich as the train went rumbling through—is perhaps the *only* song about Boston that most people know. . . .
>
> Scollay Square continues to hold memories for older Bostonians—and for sailors and the undergraduates who were entertained there. They are memories that are worth preserving, even if only in a street sign and an MBTA stop (*Boston Globe*, December 30, 1986).

Unfortunately, when the time came for its name to be restored, Scollay Square had to share the day. Bad weather forced the postponement of the ceremony to April 29, 1987. That was the day that Massachusetts Governor Michael Dukakis declared his candidacy for the office of president. His announcement was made on the Boston Common across from the State House, which is just three blocks up Tremont Street from Government Center. Peter Gelzinis of the *Boston Herald* found the timing of these two events irresistible material for what is my favorite column on the day. Gelzinis wrote, in part:

> Actually, it was an eclipse of sorts. Somewhere around lunchtime yesterday, the future and the past strayed in daffy alignment on Tremont Street.
>
> The future was blow-dried hair—blow-dried, razor sculpted and fluttered down over the brow the way every Jack Kennedy clone has worn it for the last 25 years.
>
> The past was silver strands soaked with Vitalis, neatly parted and slicked straight

back — no hair hiding the ears or creeping down over the collar, a manly man's "barber shop" cut worthy of J. Edgar Hoover and the great Curley himself.

The future was Dukakis-on-the-Common and his patented "Son of Greek Immigrant" soliloquy.

The past was Dapper O'Neil standing in Government Center, in the general vicinity of the Old Howard's grave, belting out a ragged "Bill Bailey, Please Come Home" to the tune of a honky-tonk trumpet. . . .

They were things to consider as the future rubbed elbows with the past yesterday.

Funny, but nowhere in the respective schticks did either performer try building a bridge to the other. . . .

Dap's crowd preferred the ghost of Scollay Square to Duke's vision of the future.

Dap returned to the land of Vitalis, stiptic pencils and memories of bump and grind. Memories of a less complicated, more innocent place. Memories of times before microchips and investment bankers. A time of nickel hot dogs. Memories of Scollay Square, a place that died to make way for the future (*Boston Herald*, April 30, 1987).

The renaming ceremony even made the *Herald's* sports section. The fate of the Boston Garden, built in the twenties and the home of two major sports franchises, was being decided about this time. It was generally agreed that the Garden was in dire need of either refurbishment or replacement. *Herald* columnist Joe Fitzgerald, frustrated with the city's inability to come up with a plan for the home of the Celtics and Bruins, was moved to make some comparisons with Scollay Square:

Mayor Ray Flynn spent the better part of the afternoon waxing rhapsodic about old Scollay Square at a ceremony in which he officially restored the name to what's now commonly known as Government Center. . . .

In a move that would have drawn the envy of Tempest Storm, he yanked the string that dropped a cloth which covered the sign as the crowd went wild.

Oh, get serious, Ray. How many sailors awoke from stupors to find "I Love Mom" tattooed on their buttocks following fun-filled nights at old Scollay Square? We're talking about a collection of honky-tonk joints that included a theatre popularly known as the Scratch House. *The Scratch House!* This is Hizzoner's idea of nostalgia? Good grief, we have the only mayor in America who could get sentimental over VD.

But hey, that's OK; in fact, that might even be good, because about this time next week Flynn is expected to render a decision on the fate of the Boston Garden, a bonafide mecca of history and nostalgia just a few blocks from old Scollay Square which pols and spectators are willing to scrap in their never ending pursuit of the Almighty Dollar (*Boston Herald*, April 20, 1987).

(Fitzgerald's frustration over the Garden was understandable. As a sportswriter he has probably spent as much time in that relic as any player or coach, and only recently have there been any definitive plans for the Boston Garden, which has been eluding refurbishment since Scollay Square was torn down.)

The renaming ceremony was a reunion in many ways. Most of the crowd of 3,000 or so that showed up were former West End residents who grew up near the Square. Onstage, Leon Merrian, now a successful musician, led his very own big band not far from the Red Hat and the former location of the Crawford House, places where he first made a buck. Ann Corio, still looking great more than forty years after her last performance at the Old Howard, stood on the podium next to city councillor Dapper O'Neil. Like a lot of people there, O'Neil couldn't take his eyes off her.

Standing over an original stone marker from the Old Howard (which had been lent for the occasion by the Bostonian Society), Mayor Ray Flynn read a short declaration, and after several tugs on a stubborn rope, unveiled a sign that put the name Scollay Square back on the maps of Boston.

Scollay Square Today

City Hall Plaza, though it never achieved one planner's dream of being the St. Peter's Square of Boston, has been utilized by the city for concerts, outdoor plays, Octoberfests, ethnic celebrations, even laser shows. There also seems to be a new tradition developing of holding "Appreciation Days" in the plaza for local sports franchises that reach championship play. During the summer of 1988 the Farmer's Market moved from Copley Plaza (which was being renovated), to City Hall Plaza. Open two days a week in the summer, the market represented another attempt to bring some life into the area. Yet like the rest of Government Center, it closed at the end of the day, leaving the area empty once again.

City Hall is under critical attack these days as it passes its twentieth birthday. Some city workers bemoan the lack of space, echoing a complaint made by workers in the old City Hall on School Street thirty years ago. One member of the city council has even called for the razing of the building, citing its uselessness and cramped quarters. Ideas for Government Center's rejuvenation began cropping up in the eighties. One architect suggested that a row of buildings be constructed along Cambridge Street, more or less like the ones that used to stand there. On the upper floors the city would have extra office space while the first floor would house stores, restaurants, and entertainment. Not only would this breathe life into an area that dies every day at quitting time, but the buildings would create a shield from the wind that occasionally creates a hazard for pedestrians. Another idea dealt directly with City Hall's giant inner atrium. Why not enclose it with a skylight, one citizen suggested, thus creating a weatherproof area where a restaurant could operate?

Boston's Future and the Lessons of Government Center

Today, the upcoming depression of the Central Artery, combined with the Mid-Town Cultural District renewal plan (which would, besides rejuvenating that section of the city, wipe out the last vestiges of the Combat Zone, Boston's failed attempt to replace Scollay Square) and the possible development of the Fan Pier in South Boston, signal the beginning of an era not unlike the one in which Scollay Square was replaced by Government Center.

It would be hard to argue that the city is not better off with Government Center and the development and economic growth that it induced. Yet it still seems a shame that all that was Scollay Square had to be torn down so that Boston could rise again. Looking back, one wonders if the destruction of the Old Howard or the removal of Tremont Row and the *Liberator* building were really necessary for Government Center to succeed. Just a block toward the waterfront from Government Center is the Fanueil Hall Marketplace, a stunning example of how the new Boston can succeed without sacrificing the old. The shops and restaurants surrounding the refurbished Quincy Market draw millions of people each year, making it one of the biggest tourist attractions in the country.

Has Boston learned from Scollay Square, the West End, and other renewal projects like Quincy Market? Have losses of national treasures like the Old Howard forced us to rethink our approach to urban renewal? Will developers and politicians have complete control over the shaping of the city's landscape, or will citizen groups be able to exert enough influence to ensure that their neighborhoods survive? The next twenty years will offer the answer.

And what about the renamed Scollay Square? Whether it ever again hosts crowds of people enjoying themselves along its broad avenues will be determined by the same vision that transformed it from a worn out collection of barrooms to a center of government and commerce. My guess is that if somebody can prove that there is money to be made here, changes will occur. Until then, if you choose to walk across the plaza on a windy day, button up. It can get mighty cold out there.

BIBLIOGRAPHY

Allen, Fred, *Much Ado about Me* (Boston: Little Brown, 1956)

Bacon, Edward M., *The Book of Boston* (Boston: The Book of Boston Co., 1916)

——, *Rambles Around Old Boston* (Boston: Little Brown, 1914)

Boston City Council, *Celebration of the 250th Anniversary of the Settlement of Boston* (Boston: City Press, 1880)

Boston Transit Commission, *Annual Report* (Boston: Boston City Printers, 1896, 1897, 1898, 1899, 1923, 1925)

Bruce, Robert, *Bell: Alexander Graham Bell and the Conquest of Solitude* (Boston: Little, Brown, 1973)

Buni, Andrew, and Alan Rogers, *Boston, City on a Hill* (Woodland Hills, CA: Windsor Publications, 1984)

Corio, Ann, *This Was Burlesque* (New York: Holt Reinhart, 1968)

Curley, James Michael, *I'd Do It Again* (Englewood Cliffs, New Jersey: Prentice Hall, 1957)

Drake, Samuel Adams, *Old Landmarks and Historic Personages of Boston* (Cambridge, Massachusetts: University Press, 1900)

Geis, Joseph and Francis, *The Ingenious Yankees* (New York: Thomas Y. Crowell, 1976)

Hale, Edward Everett, *Historic Boston and Its Neighborhoods* (New York: D. Appleton & Co., 1898)

Harris, John, *Historic Walks In Old Boston* (Chester, Connecticut: Pequot Press, 1982)

Hentoff, Nat, *Boston Boy* (New York: Alfred A. Knopf, 1932)

Herlihy, Elisabeth M., *Fifty Years of Boston: A Memorial Volume* (Boston: Boston Tercentenary Committee, 1932)

History of Boston from 1630 to 1856 (Boston: F. C. Moore, 1856)

Jones, Howard, *The Many Voices of Boston* (Boston: Little Brown)

Kay, Jane Holtz, *Lost Boston* (Boston: Houghton Mifflin, 1980)

King, Moses, *How to See Boston: A Trustworthy Guide Book* (Boston: Macullar, Parker & Company, 1895)

Kirker, Harold and James, *Bullfinch's Boston* (New York: Oxford University Press, 1964)

Lynch, Kevin, *The Image of the City* (Cambridge, Massachusetts: MIT Press, 1959)

Lyons, A. C., *Invitation to Boston* (New York: M. Barrows & Co., 1947)

Mann, Albert W., *Walks and Talks About Historic Boston* (Boston: Mann Publishing, 1916)

Martin, William, *Back Bay* (New York: Pocket Books, 1979)

Marx, Harpo, *Harpo Speaks* (New York: Bernard Geis Associates, 1961)

McGuirk, Kathleen L., *The Diary of Thomas A. Edison* (Old Greenwich, Connecticut: Chatham Press, 1968)

Norton, Elliot, *Broadway Down East* (Boston: Trustees of the Boston Public Library, 1978)

O'Connor, Thomas H., *Bibles, Brahmins and Bosses: A Short History of Boston* (Boston: Trustees of the Boston Public Library, 1984)

Porter, Alexander, *Changes in Value of Real Estate in Boston*, Vol. #1, No. 3 (Boston: Bostonian Society, 1888)

——, *The Scollays* (Boston: Bostonian Society, 1906)

Ross, Marjorie Drake, *The Book of Boston* (New York: Hastings House, 1968)

Rossiter, William S., *Days and Ways in Old Boston* (Boston: R. H. Stearns, 1915)

Russell, Francis, *A City in Terror 1919: The Boston Police Strike* (New York: Viking, 1975)

Savage, Edward, *Police Recollections or Boston by Daylight and Gaslight* (Boston: John P. Doyle, 1873)

Schiff, Pearl, *Scollay Square* (New York: Reinhart, 1952)

Silverberg, Robert, *Light for the World: Edison and the Power Industry* (Princeton, New Jersey: D. Van Nostrand, 1967)

Sothern, Georgia, *My Life in Burlesque: An Autobiography* (New York: Signet, 1972)

Stark, James H., *Stark's Antique Views of Boston* (Boston: James A. Stark)

Thwing, Annie Haven, *The Crooked & Narrow Streets of the Town of Boston* (Boston: Marshall Jones, 1920)

Warden, G. B., *Boston: 1689–1776* (Boston: Little Brown, 1970)

Weston, George F., Jr, *Boston Ways: High, By and Folk* (Boston: Beacon Press, 1957)

Whitehill, Walter Muir, *The Metamorphosis of Scollay and Bowdoin Squares* (Boston: Bostonian Society, 1973)

——, ed. *Boston: A Topographical History* (Cambridge, Massachusetts: Harvard University Press, 1968)

Widener, Don, *Lemmon: A Biography* (New York: Macmillan, 1975)

Winsor, Justin, *Memorial History of Boston, vols. I-IV* (Boston: James R. Osgood, 1881)

OTHER SOURCES

M. E. Nichols, *American City* 40:151, April 1929
"Boston to Build Largest Firehouse in the Country"

American City 69:106–7, June 3, 1954
"Great Forces at Work for Civic Betterment"

S. H. Holbrook, *American Mercury* 58:411–16, April 1944
"Boston's Temple of Burlesque"

S. H. Holbrook, *American Mercury* 59:416–21, October 1944
"Boston's Scollay Square"

Architectural Forum 120:79–87, June 1964
"Boston: Rebuilding a City"

Architectural Record 139:140–141, June 1966
"Plaza Deal for Boston's Government Center"

Bay State Librarian, July 1963
"A Plea for Cornhill"

Business Week 90ff December 19, 1959
"Boston's Bond Rating Slips a Notch"

Business Week 112–6, June 9, 1962
"Boom Moves into the Hub"

Business Week, April 13, 1963
"Old Boston Spruces Up"

G. Manning, *Colliers* 126:22–123ff, September 30, 1950
"Always Something Doing at Boston's Old Howard"

Dodge News Magazine 23:9

Economist (9330.542) 952, March 11, 1961
"The Battle for Boston"

Fortune 55:286ff June 1957
"Is Boston Beginning to Boil?"

Fortune 69:132–137, June 1964
"Boston: What Can a Sick City Do"

Harper's Weekly 39:114, February 2, 1895
"Boston from the Ames Building"

C. L. Pollack, *Harper's Weekly* 53:11–12, August 21, 1909

New Republic 58:327–29, May 8, 1929
"Boston Stays Pure"

W. Von Eckardt, *New Republic*, 149:15–19, September 14, 1963

Newsweek 58:25, July 3, 1961
"The 'Old Harvard' "

R. T. Bushnell, *North American Review* 229:518–25, May 1930
"Banned in Boston"

Saturday Evening Post 232:10, September 26, 1959
"Boston's Old Howard Burlesque House Would Make a New Type National Shrine"

Time 84:60ff., November 6, 1964
"Under the Knife, or All for Their Own Good"

U.S. News and World Report 57:52–54, September 21, 1964
"Boston Makes a Comeback"

Newspapers: *Boston Evening Record, Boston Evening Transcript, Boston Globe, Boston Herald, Boston Post, Boston Record-American, Boston Traveler*

The West End Branch of the Boston Public Library interviews were recorded and transcribed by Paul Cincotta.